101 Cartoons

Joe McKeever

Parson's Porch

Parson's Porch Books

101 Cartoons

ISBN: Softcover 978-1-936912-93-3

Copyright © 2014 by Joe McKeever

To order additional copies of this book, contact:

Parson's Porch Books
1-423-475-7308
www.parsonsporch.com

Parson's Porch Books is an imprint of Parson's Porch & Company (PP&C) in Cleveland, Tennessee. PP&C is an innovative non-profit organization which raises money by publishing books of noted authors, representing all genres. All donations from contributors and profits from publishing are shared with the poor.

FROM JOE MCKEEVER....

When I was five years old, my mother sat me down at the kitchen table with my little sister Carolyn, gave us pencil and paper, and said, "Now draw!" She was not attempting to teach us anything, but merely trying to get us out of the way while she did her housework.

And, that's how I discovered that I love to draw. The next year, when I started to the first grade at Nauvoo (AL) Elementary School, the other children would gather around and watch me draw. To this day, I can outdraw any group of first-graders you will ever meet.

For over forty years, while pastoring churches and living the life of a Baptist minister, I've drawn cartoons for religious publications, mostly within our Southern Baptist Convention. These days, and for the past decade or more, the Baptist Press website posts one of our drawings each weekday. (See them at www.bpnews.net/cartoons)

Most of these cartoons have been featured on that website and in various publications. I am pleased we can present this collection of 101 of the most recent drawings. We send them forth with the prayer they will bring a smile to your heart and a lift to your spirit.

"In thy presence there is fullness of joy..." (Psalm 16:11)

New Orleans, Louisiana
March 2014
Website: www.joemckeever.com
Email: joe@joemckeever.com
And, we're on Facebook!

"NOT YET, FRIEND! THE PASTOR IS TAKING ME FISHING NEXT WEEK."

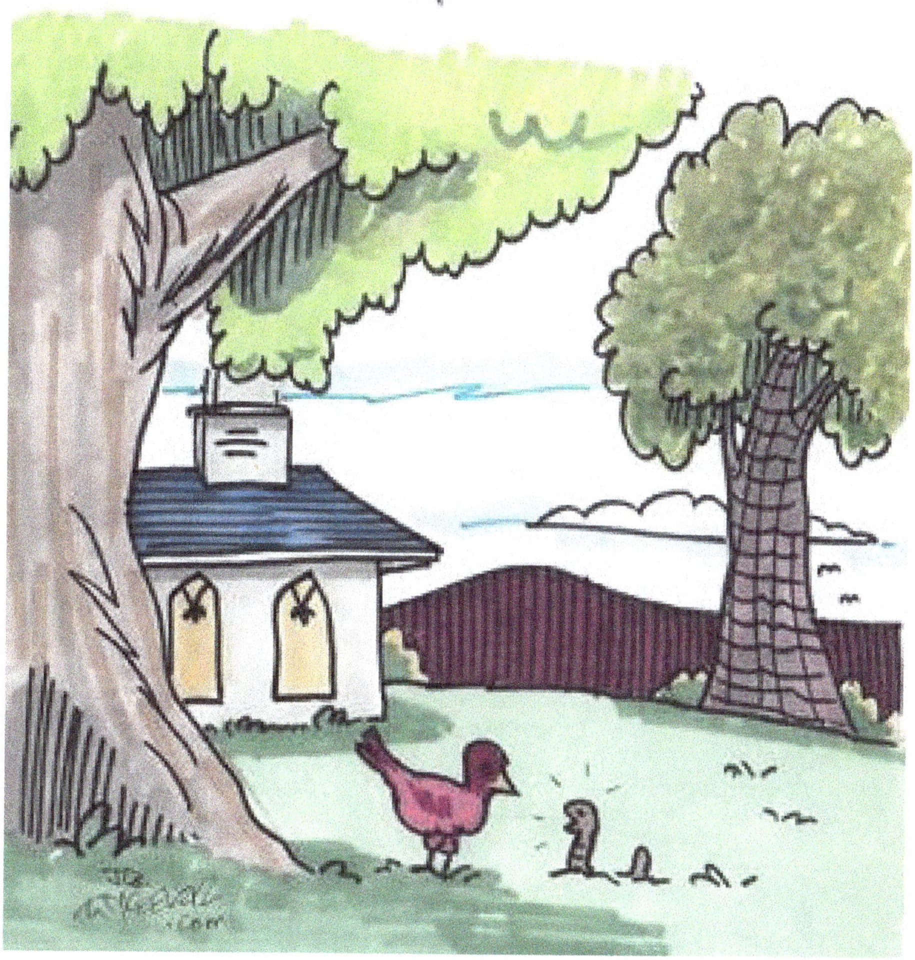

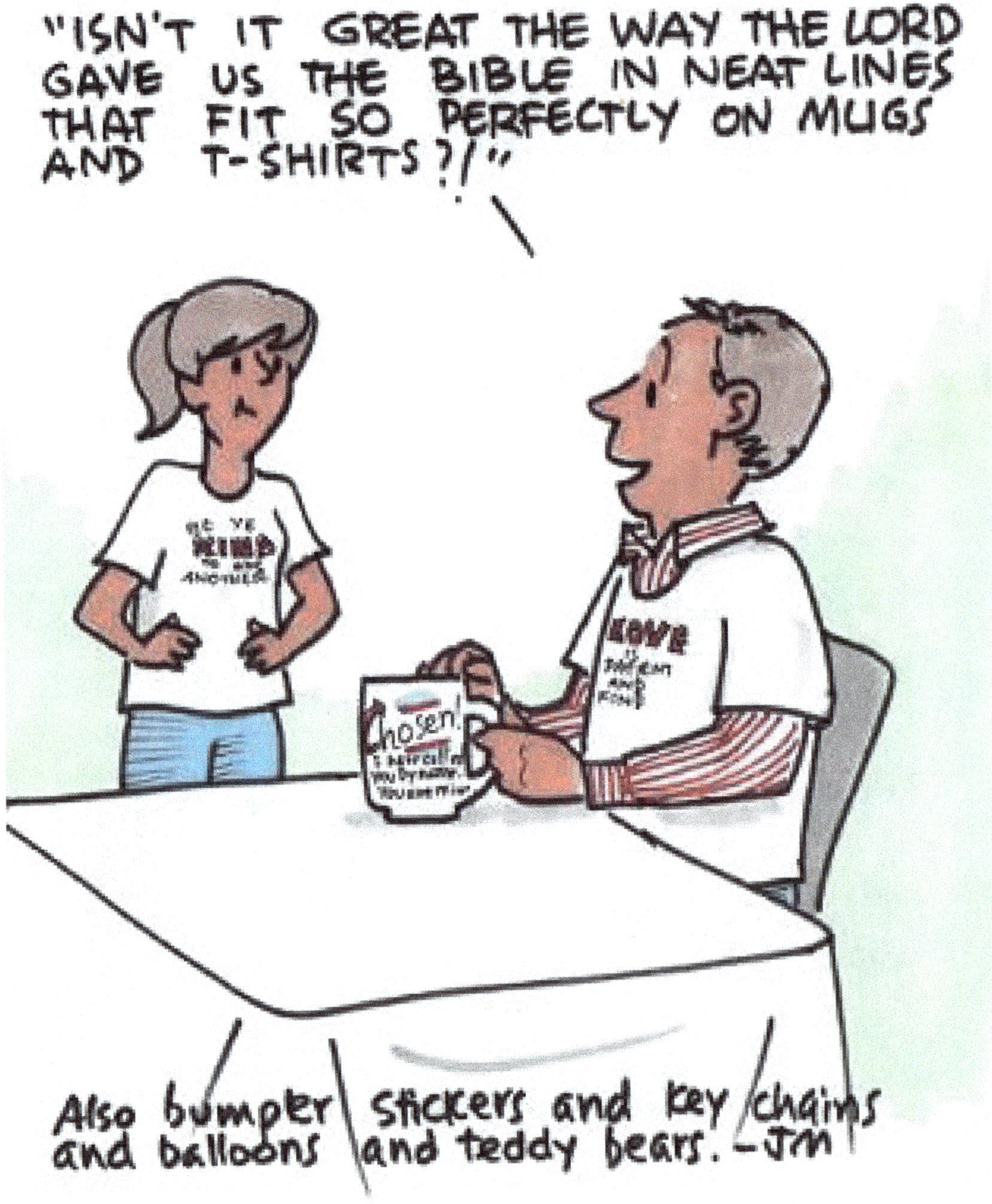
"ISN'T IT GREAT THE WAY THE LORD GAVE US THE BIBLE IN NEAT LINES THAT FIT SO PERFECTLY ON MUGS AND T-SHIRTS?!"
LOVE
Chosen!
Also bumper stickers and key chains and balloons and teddy bears. –JM

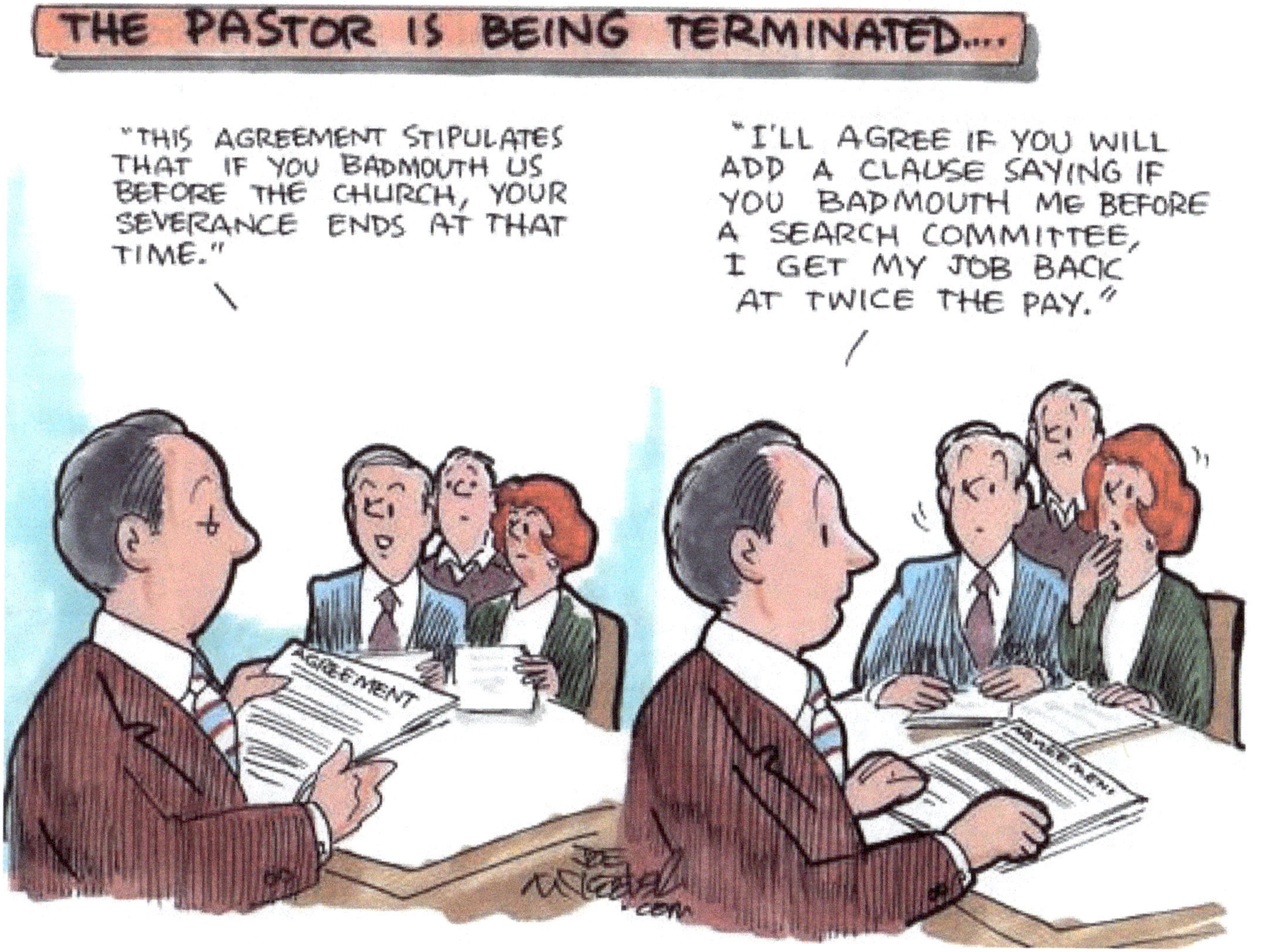
THE PASTOR IS BEING TERMINATED....
"THIS AGREEMENT STIPULATES THAT IF YOU BADMOUTH US BEFORE THE CHURCH, YOUR SEVERANCE ENDS AT THAT TIME."
"I'LL AGREE IF YOU WILL ADD A CLAUSE SAYING IF YOU BADMOUTH ME BEFORE A SEARCH COMMITTEE, I GET MY JOB BACK AT TWICE THE PAY."
AGREEMENT

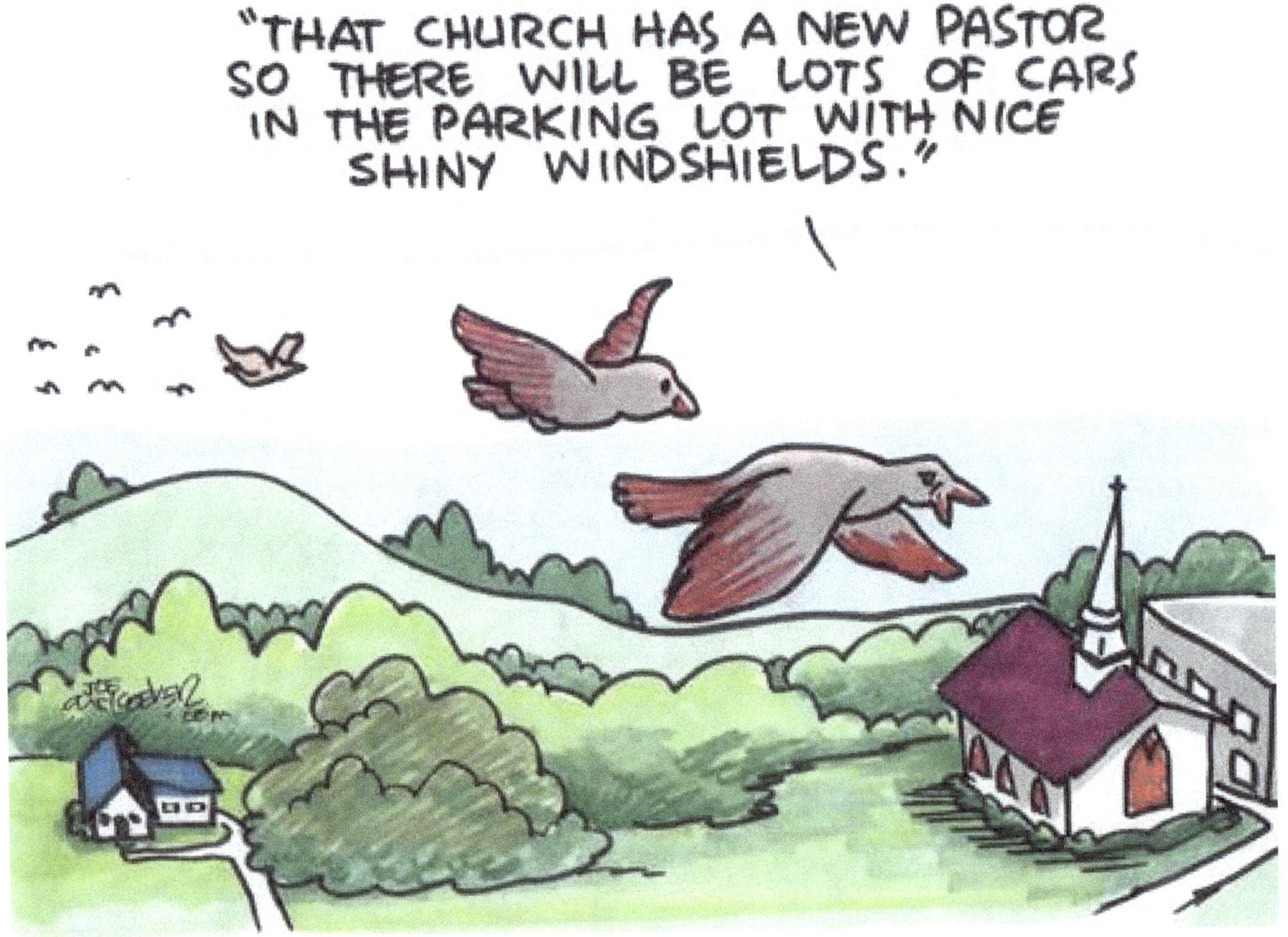
"THAT CHURCH HAS A NEW PASTOR SO THERE WILL BE LOTS OF CARS IN THE PARKING LOT WITH NICE SHINY WINDSHIELDS."

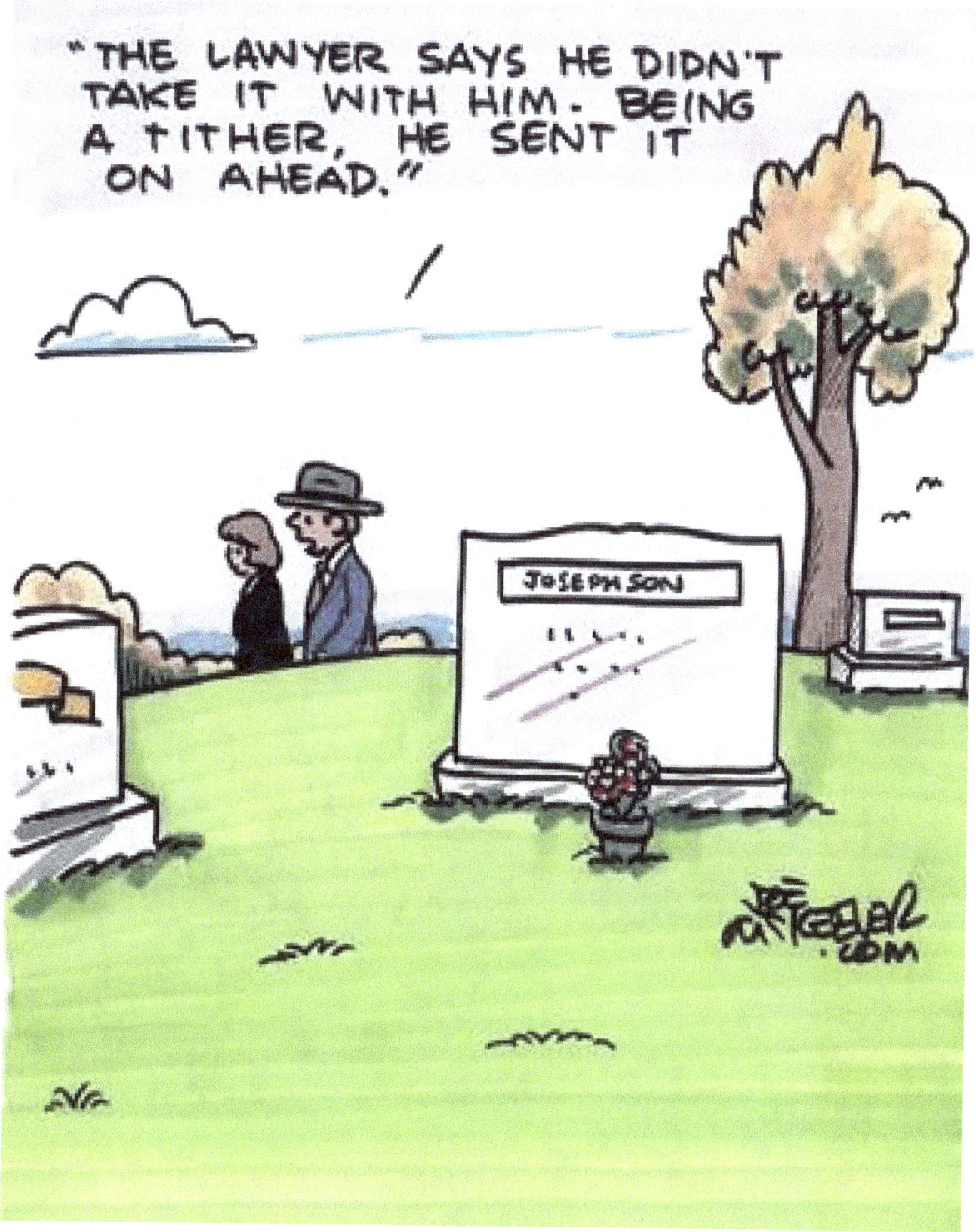
"THE LAWYER SAYS HE DIDN'T TAKE IT WITH HIM. BEING A TITHER, HE SENT IT ON AHEAD."
JOSEPHSON

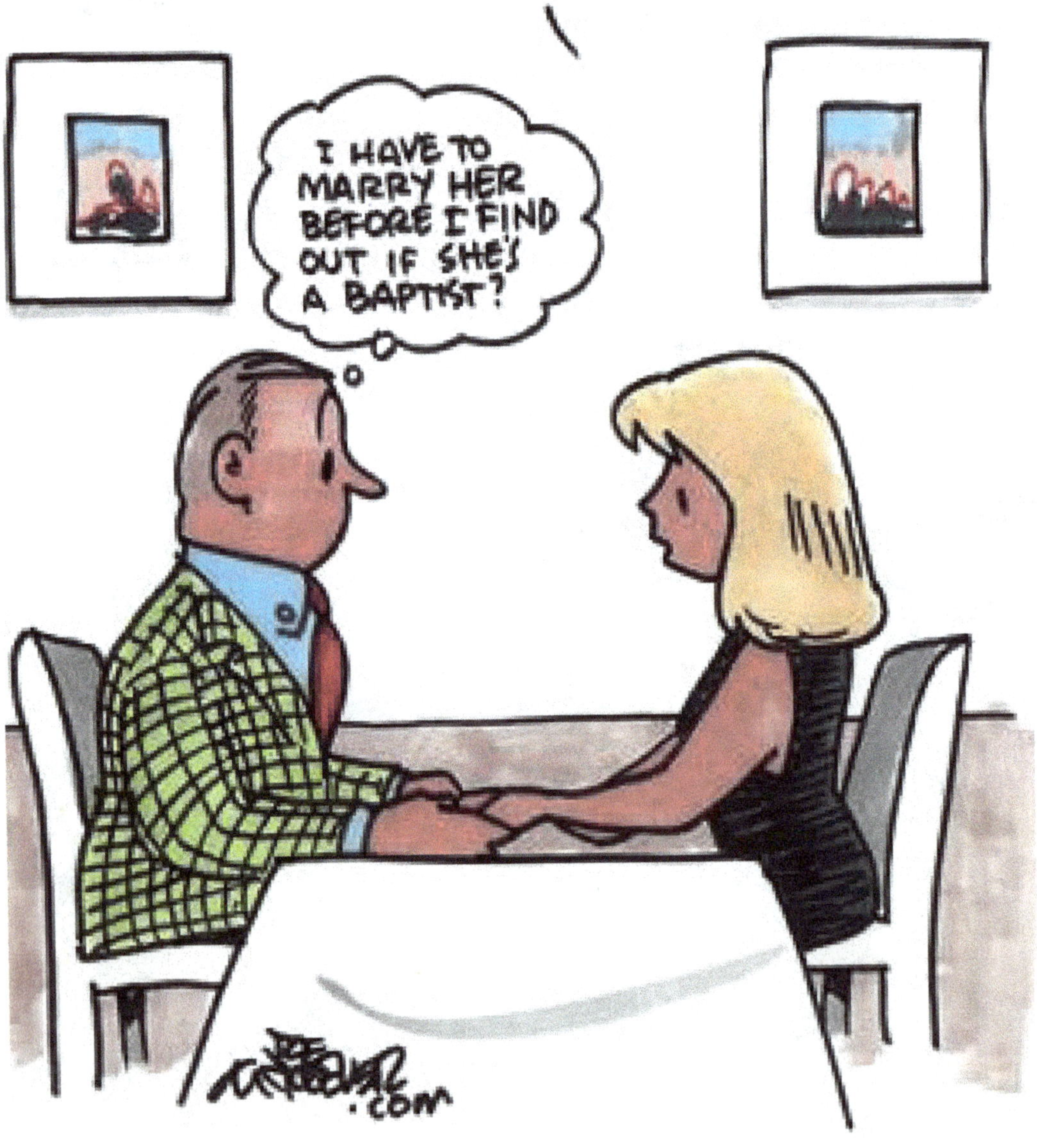
I HAVE TO MARRY HER BEFORE I FIND OUT IF SHE'S A BAPTIST?

"I NEVER DISCUSS RELIGION OR POLITICS UNTIL THE TRUST LEVEL HAS BEEN SHOWN TO BE SOLID AND HIGH."

"AND LORD, PLEASE GIVE ME A SMILE LIKE JOEL OSTEEN... OR MAYBE HIS HAIR... AND A WIFE LIKE HIS. OOPS. STRIKE THAT, LORD!"

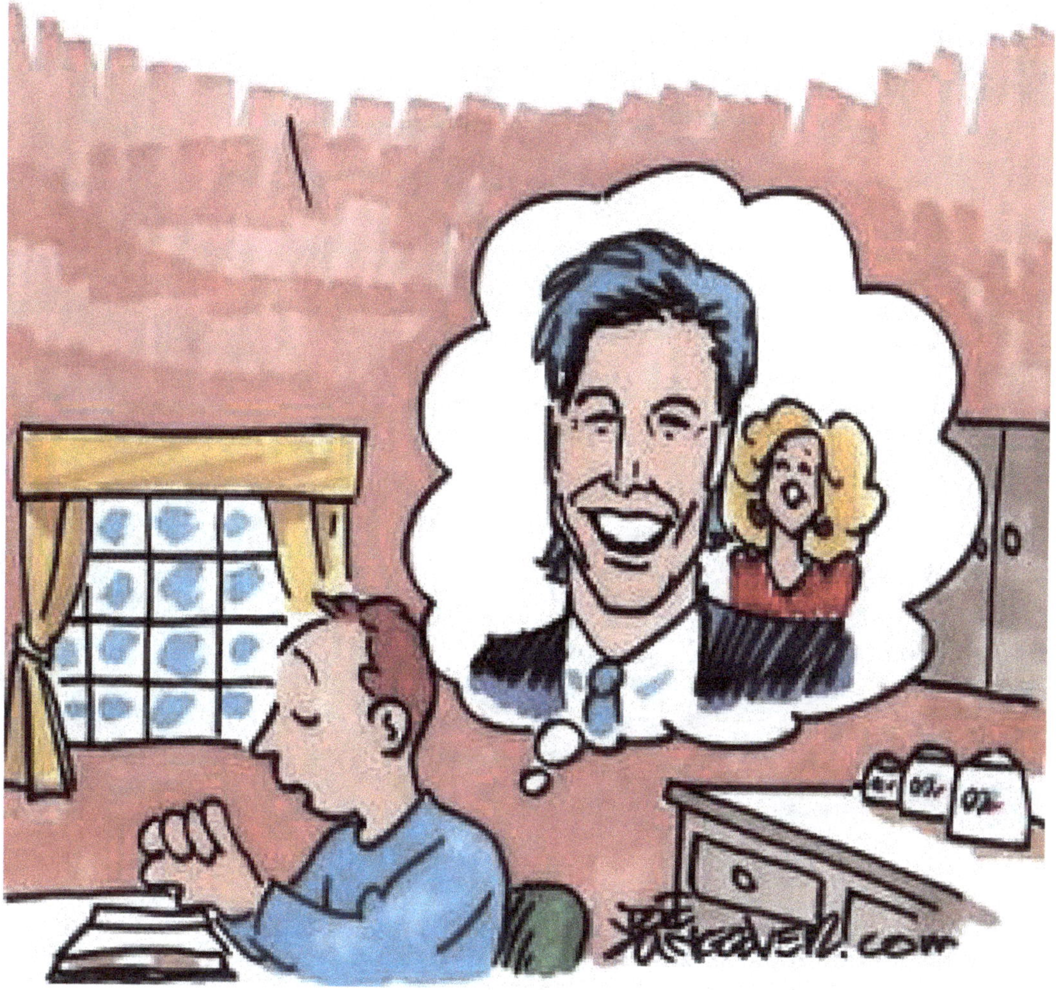

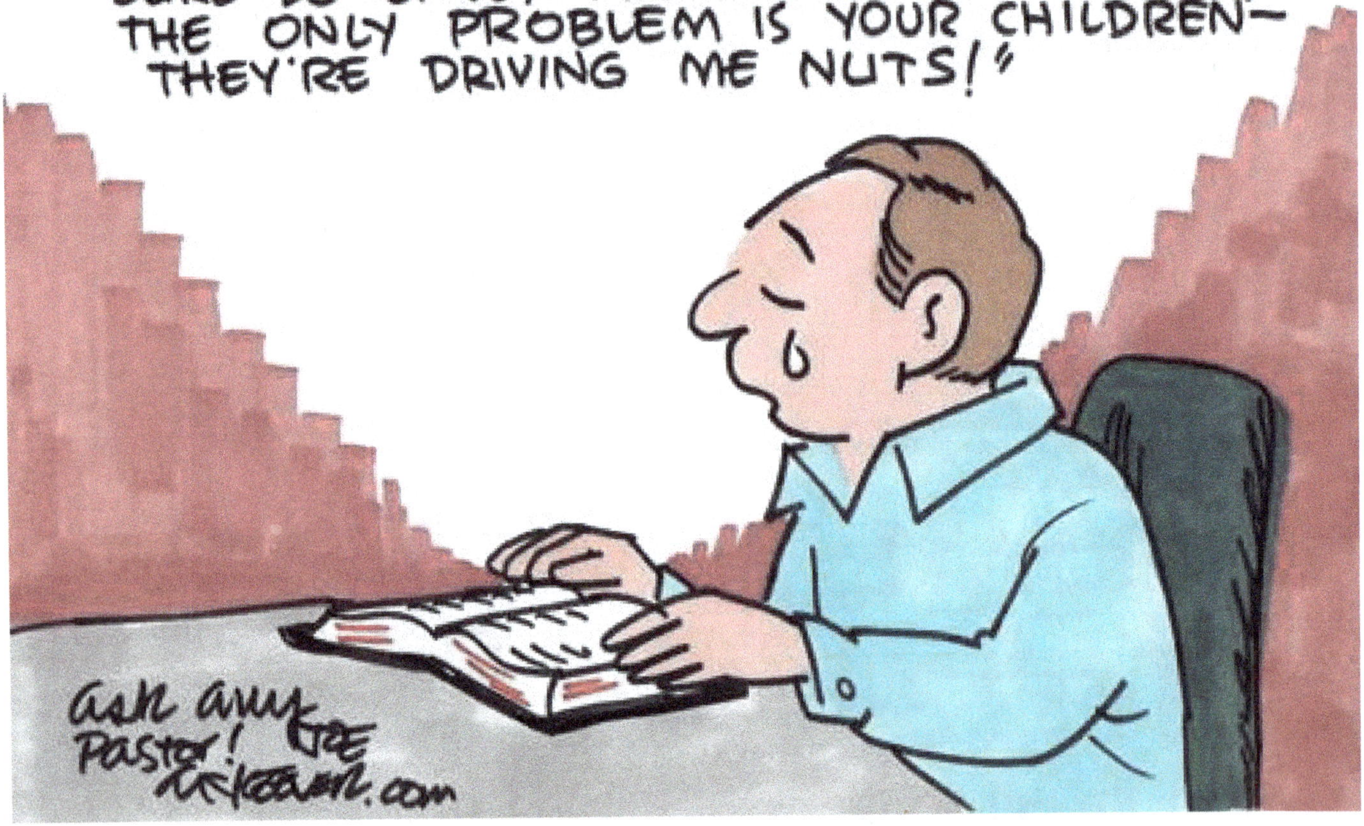
ask any Pastor!
JOE McKeever.com

"DEAR LORD, THANK YOU FOR CALLING ME INTO THE MINISTRY. I LOVE THY CHURCH, I TREASURE YOUR WORD, AND SURE DO ENJOY PREACHING. BUT FATHER, THE ONLY PROBLEM IS YOUR CHILDREN— THEY'RE DRIVING ME NUTS!"

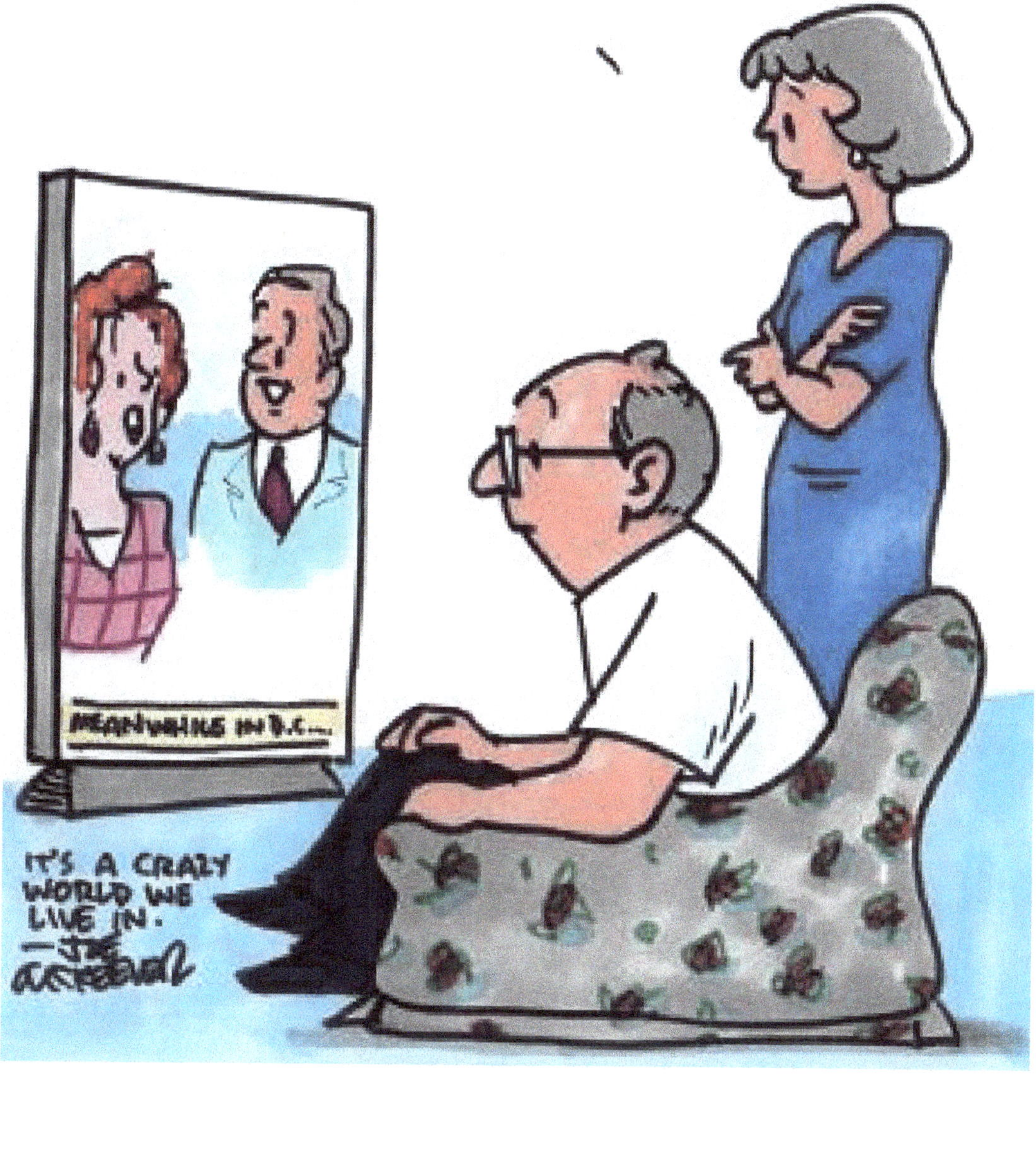
IT'S A CRAZY WORLD WE LIVE IN.
—JOE

"LET'S NOT TELL PEOPLE WE WATCH THIS NEWS CHANNEL. IT' MAKES US SEEM OLD AND CAUSES THEM TO LOSE ADVERTISERS."

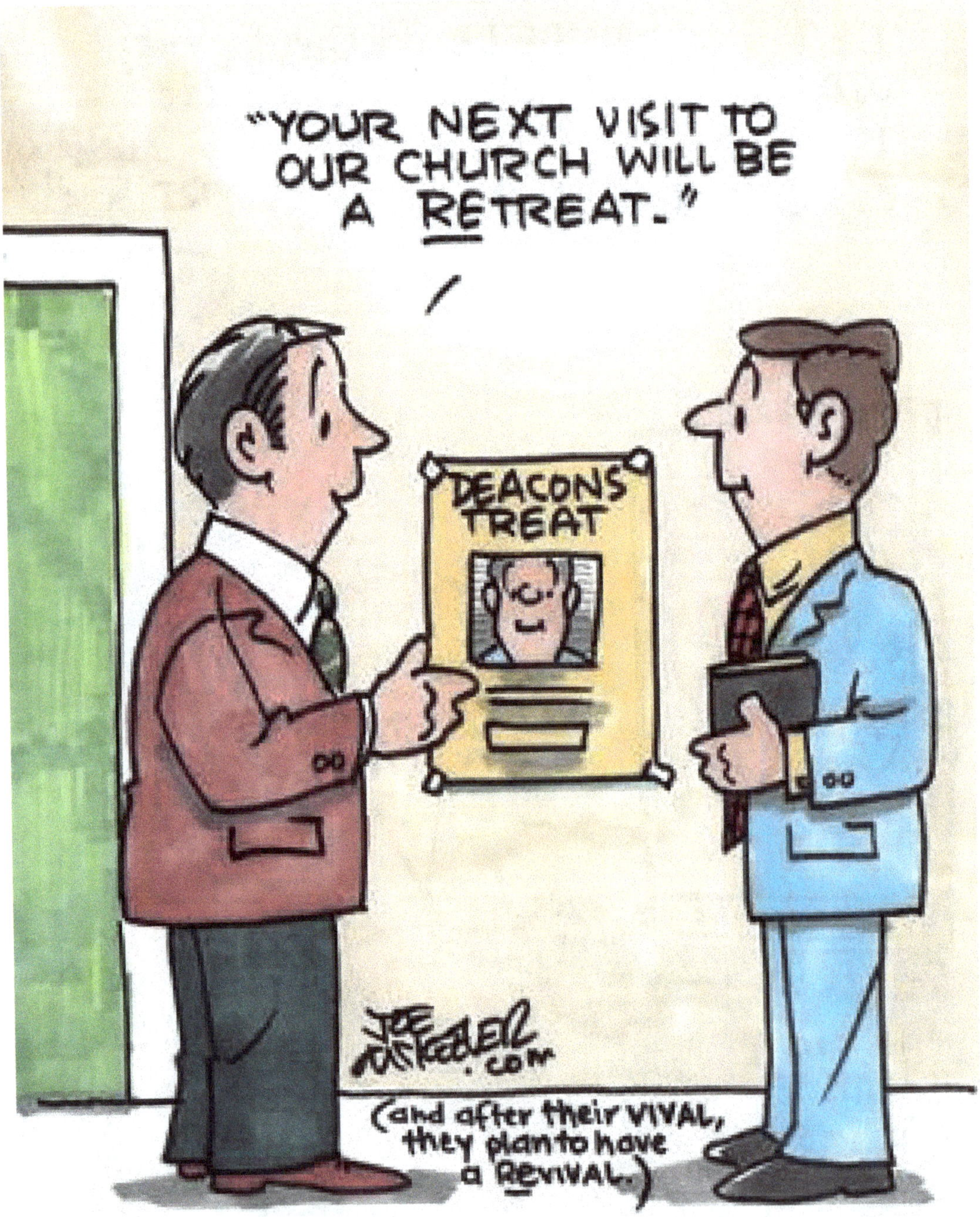
"YOUR NEXT VISIT TO
OUR CHURCH WILL BE
A RETREAT."
DEACONS
TREAT
JOE
McKEEVER
.COM
(and after their VIVAL,
they plan to have
a REVIVAL.)

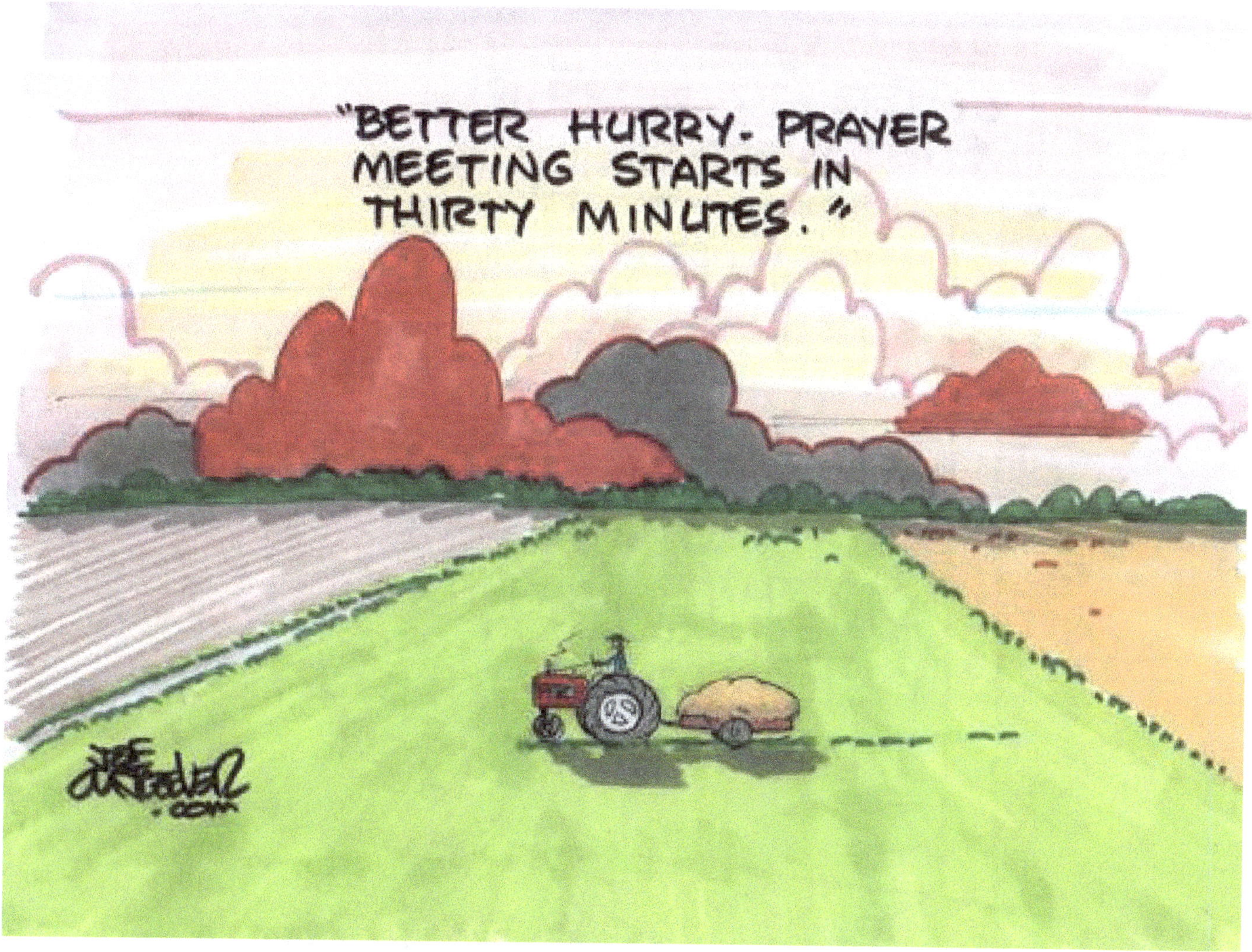
"BETTER HURRY. PRAYER MEETING STARTS IN THIRTY MINUTES."

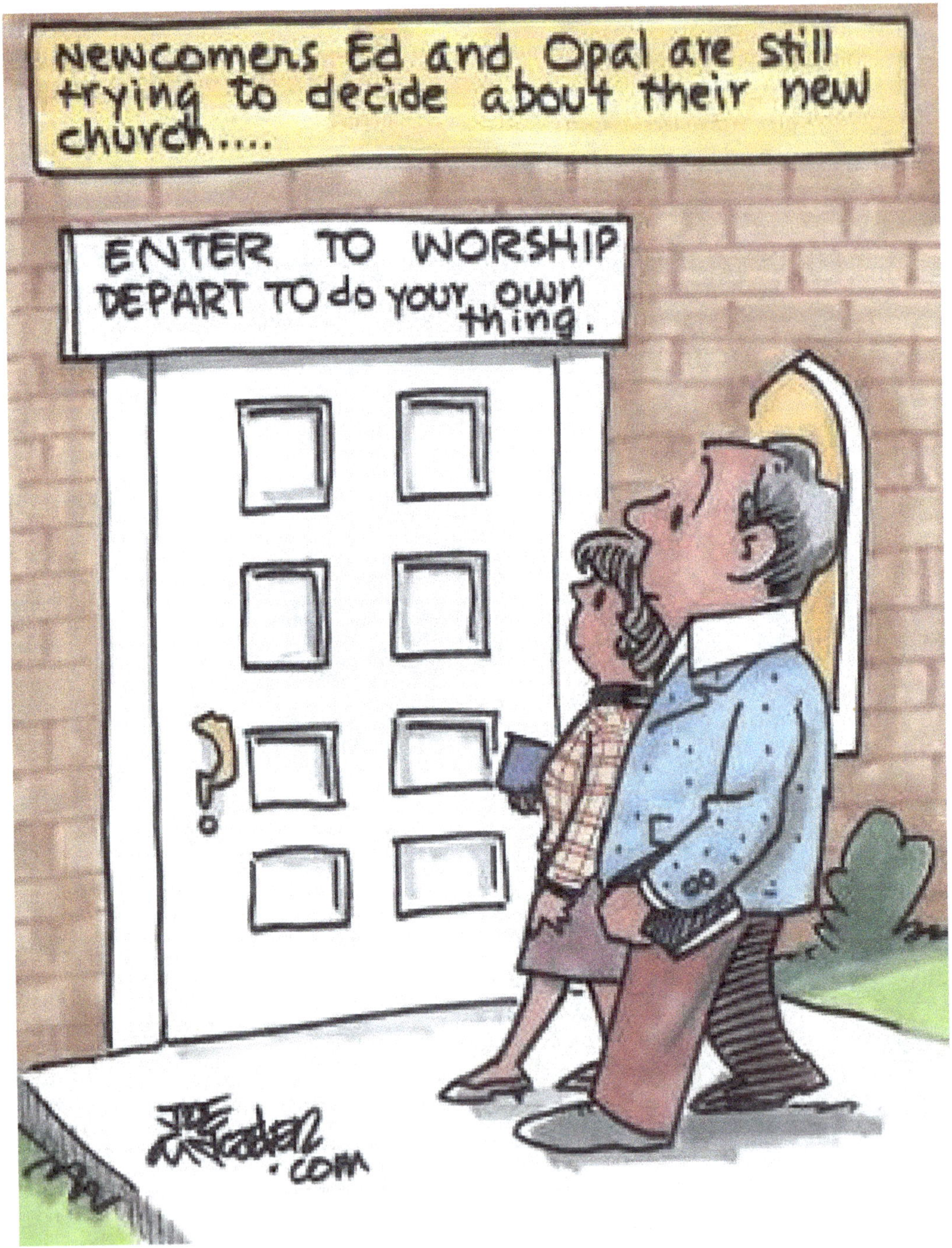
Newcomers Ed and Opal are still trying to decide about their new church....
ENTER TO WORSHIP
DEPART TO do your own thing.
JOE McKEEVER.com

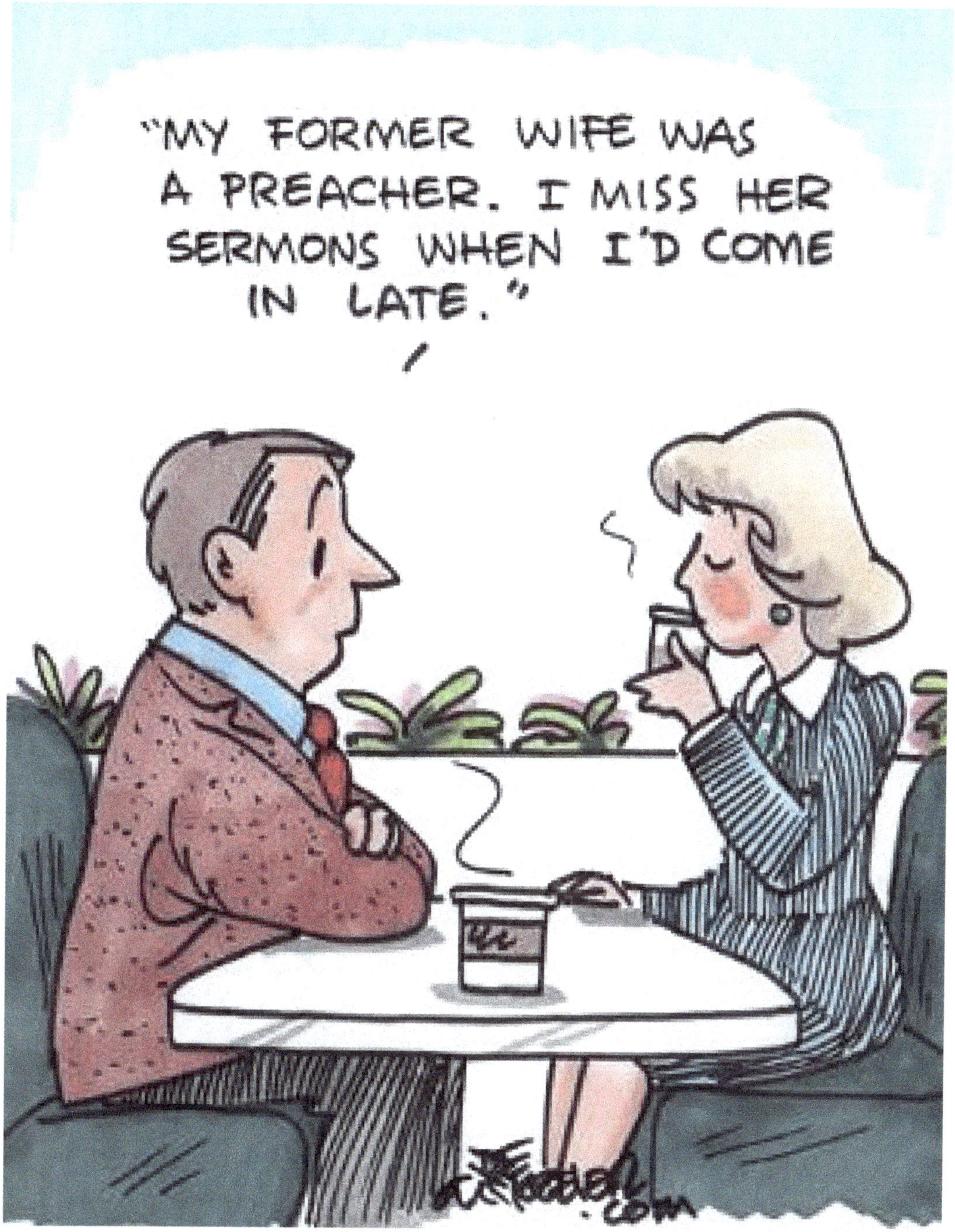
"MY FORMER WIFE WAS A PREACHER. I MISS HER SERMONS WHEN I'D COME IN LATE."

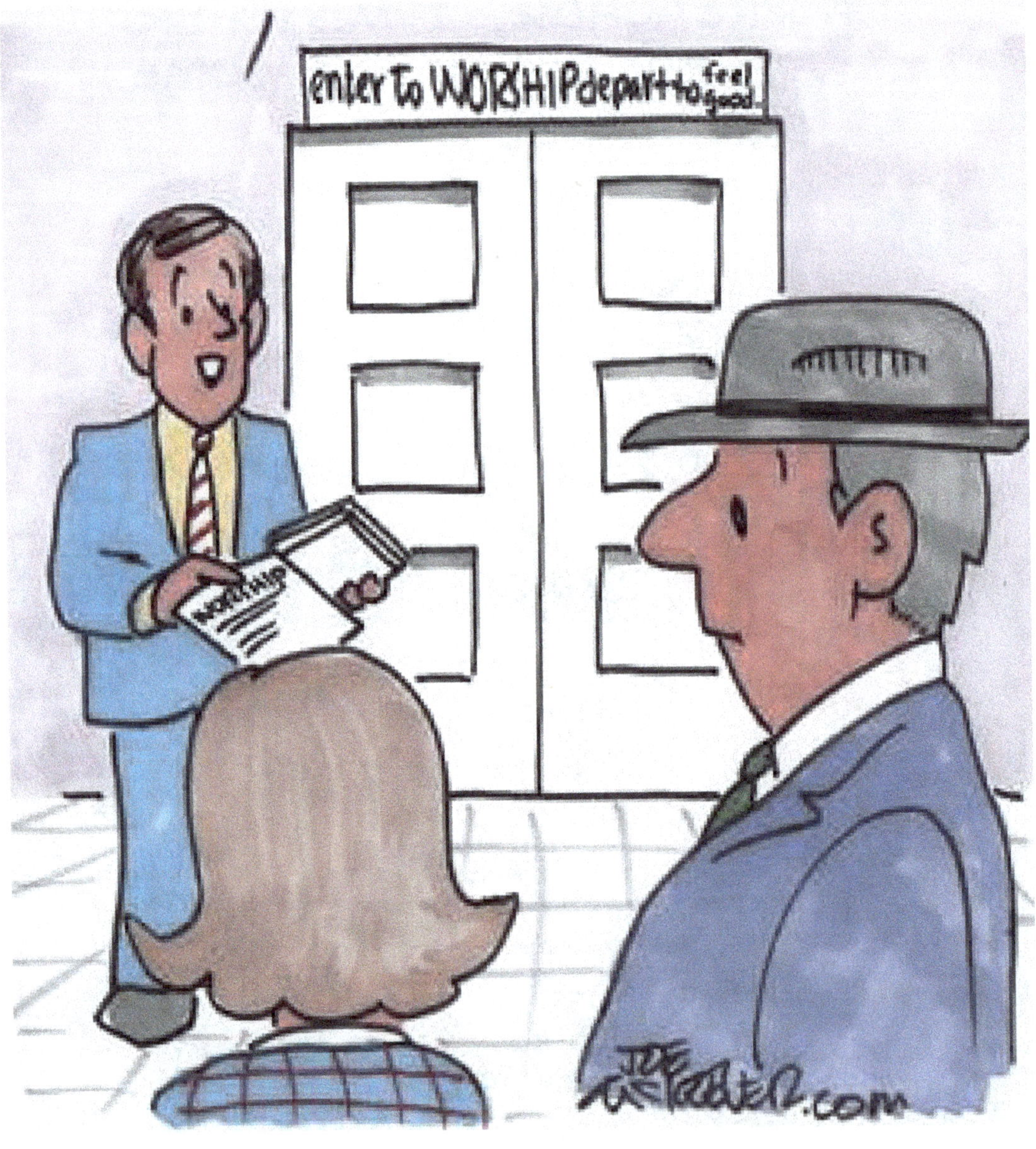
enter to WORSHIP depart to feel good.
WORSHIP

"GOOD MORNING! WELCOME TO THE CHURCH OF GOOD SOLVENCY! $25 PLEASE, UNLESS YOU ARE A TITHING MEMBER. DEBIT CARDS ACCEPTED."

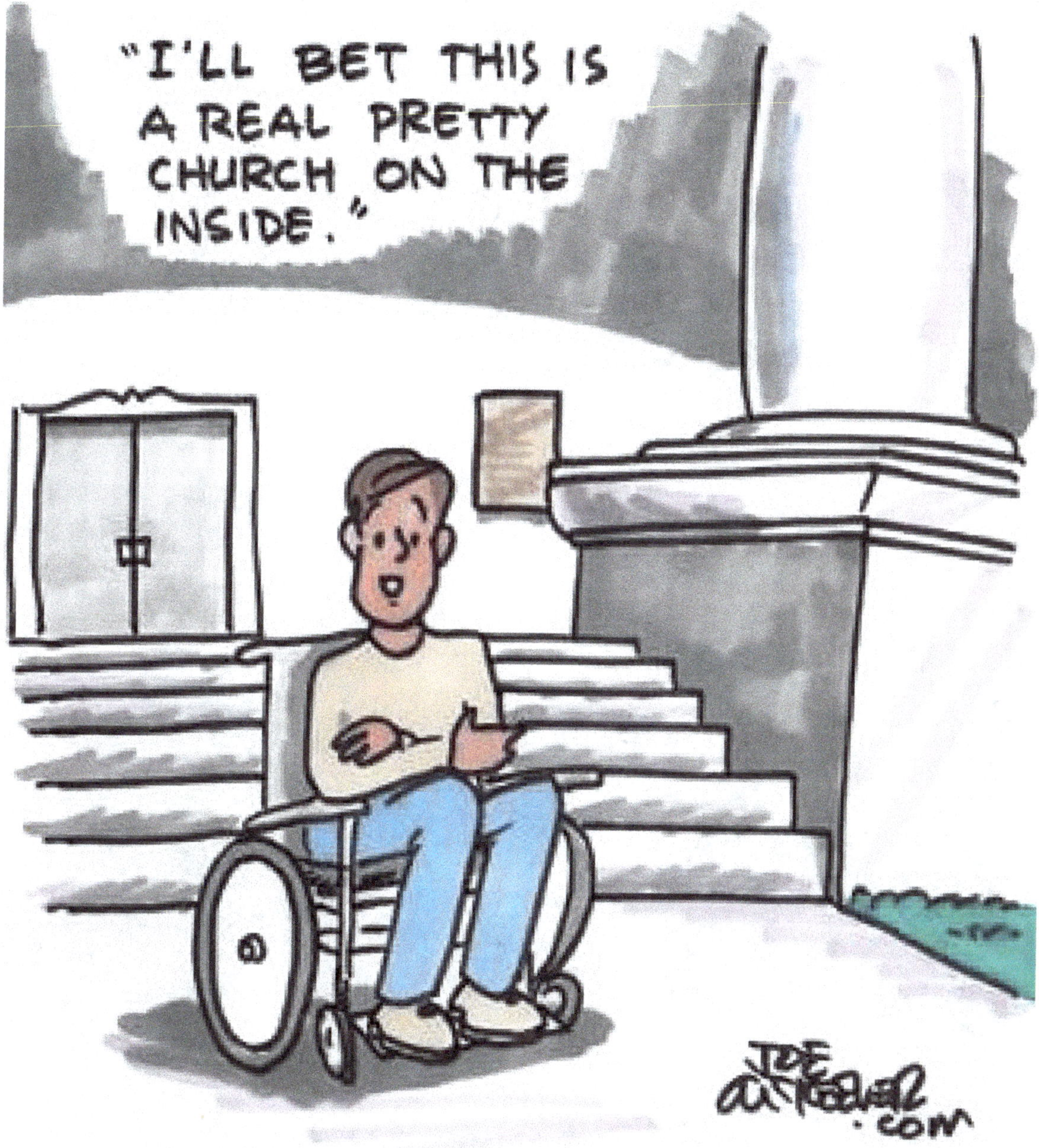
"I'LL BET THIS IS A REAL PRETTY CHURCH ON THE INSIDE."
JOE KOELKER.com

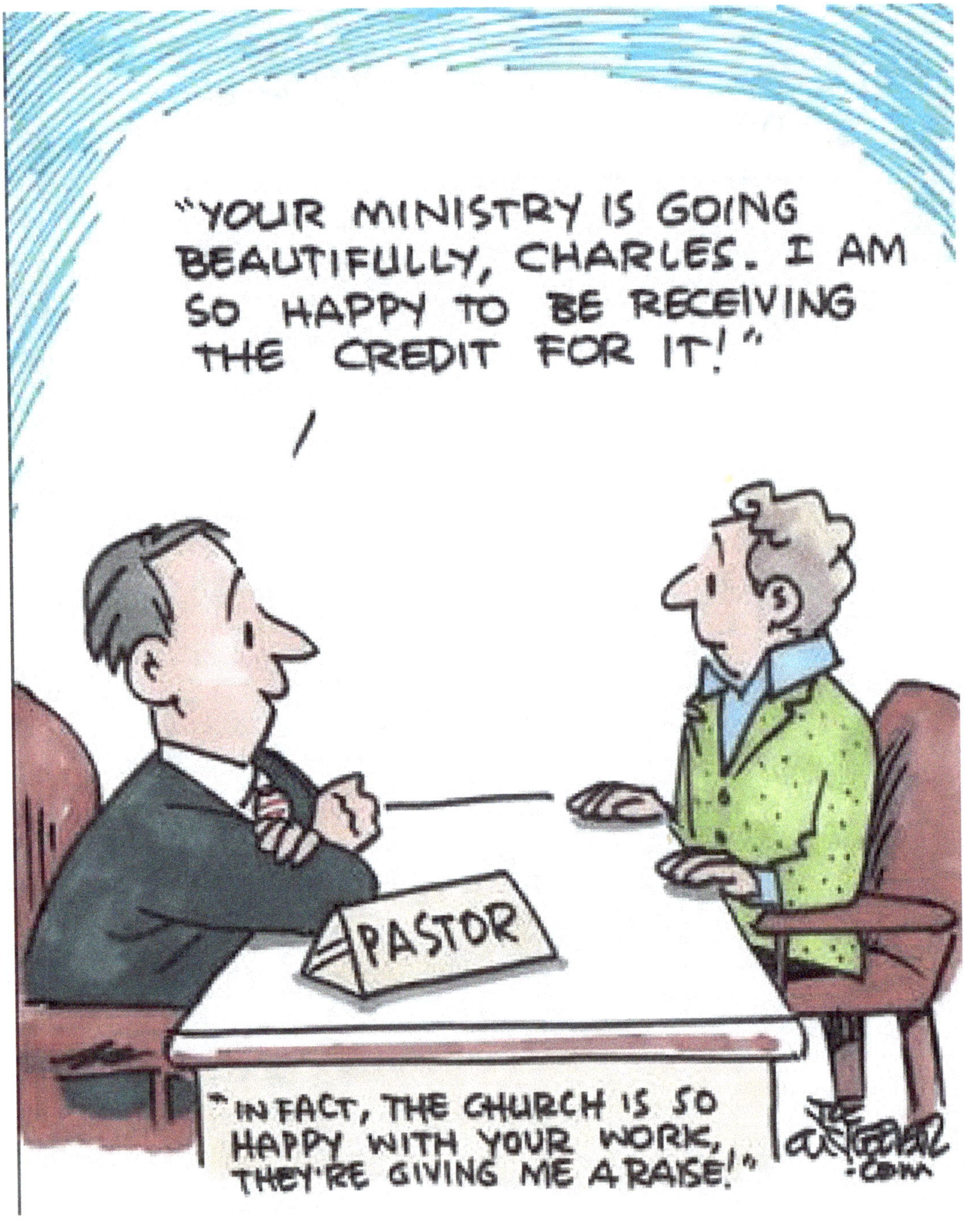
"YOUR MINISTRY IS GOING BEAUTIFULLY, CHARLES. I AM SO HAPPY TO BE RECEIVING THE CREDIT FOR IT!"
PASTOR
"IN FACT, THE CHURCH IS SO HAPPY WITH YOUR WORK, THEY'RE GIVING ME A RAISE!"

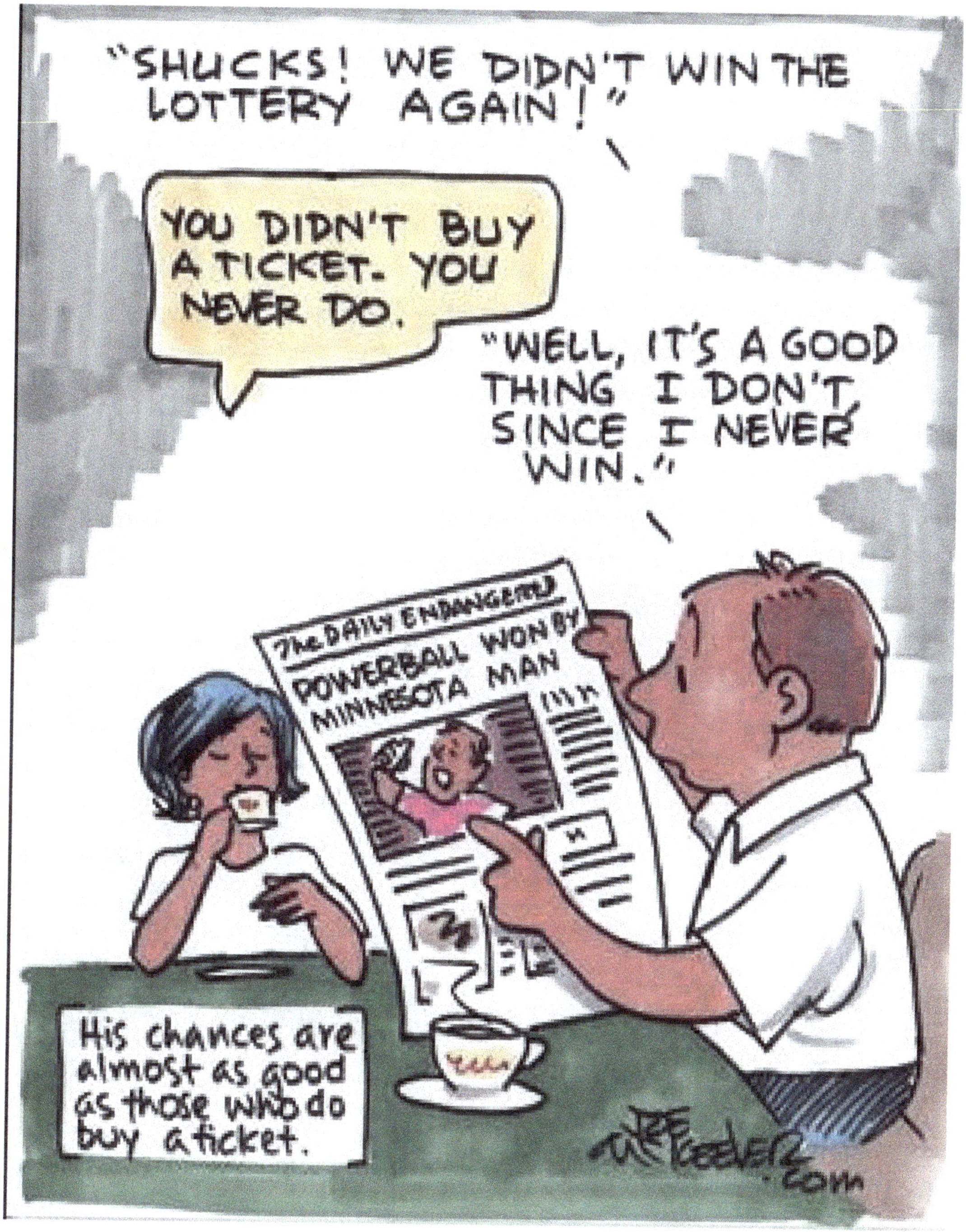
"SHUCKS! WE DIDN'T WIN THE LOTTERY AGAIN!"
YOU DIDN'T BUY A TICKET. YOU NEVER DO.
"WELL, IT'S A GOOD THING I DON'T, SINCE I NEVER WIN."
The DAILY ENDANGERED
POWERBALL WON BY MINNESOTA MAN
His chances are almost as good as those who do buy a ticket.

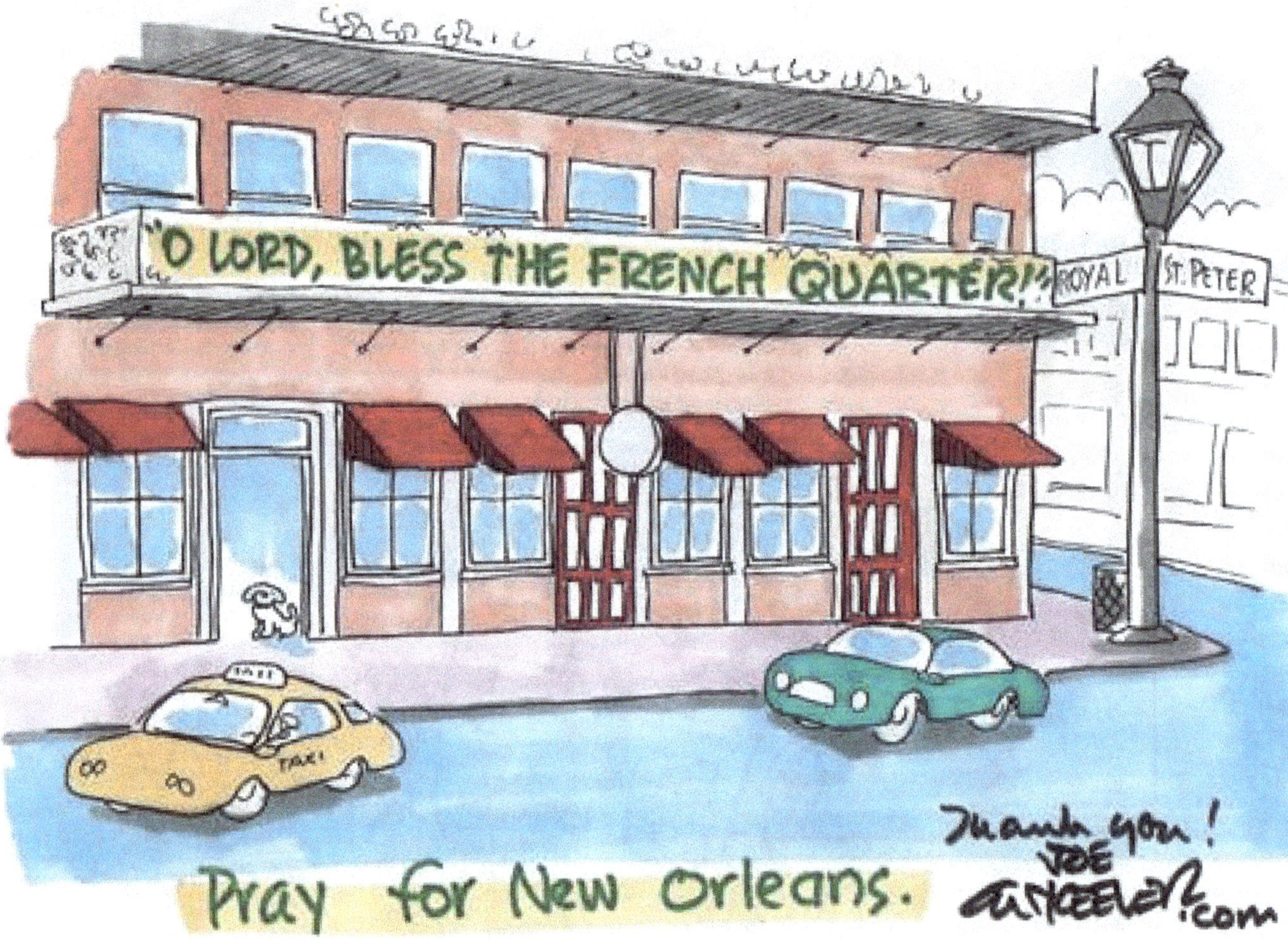
"O LORD, BLESS THE FRENCH QUARTER!"
ROYAL
ST. PETER
Pray for New Orleans.
Thank you!
JOE
McKEEVER.com

"I'M THANKFUL FOR YOU, THANKFUL ALL OUR CHILDREN ARE GROWN AND HAVE JOBS, AND ESPECIALLY THANKFUL I'M GETTING CLOSE TO THE AGE WHEN I CAN QUIT MY JOB AND LET THE KIDS ALL SUPPORT US FOR A CHANGE!"
UH OH. NO ONE TOLD THEM THIS WAS THE PLAN.
JOE KOHLER.com

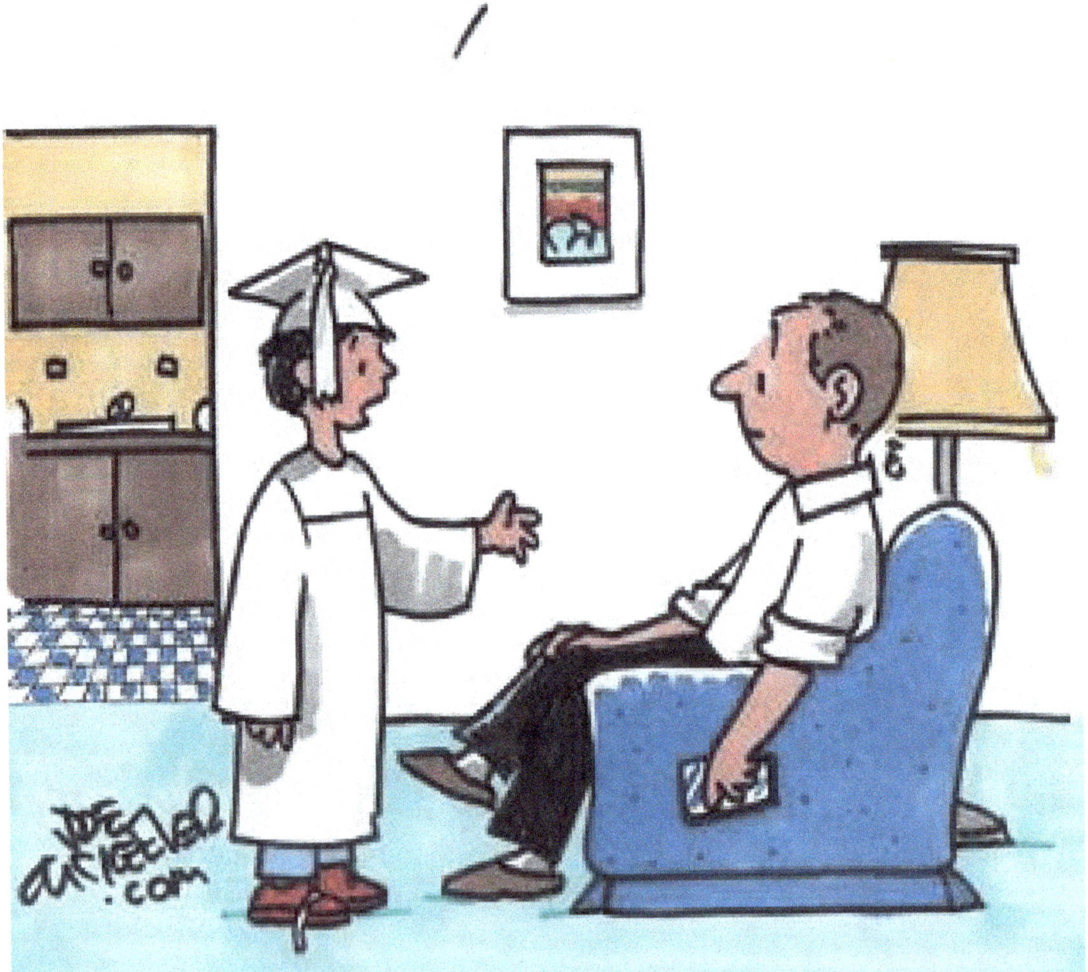

"I SHOULD BE RECEIVING MORE RESPECT AROUND HERE, POP—NOW THAT I'M AN ELEMENTARY SCHOOL GRADUATE."

"BY THE WAY, WHEN YOU'VE FOUND THE STABLE AND HAVE WORSHIPED, YOU'D BE INTERESTED TO KNOW THAT THE DINER OUT ON ROUTE 278 SERVES THE BEST COFFEE TO BE HAD ANYWHERE!"

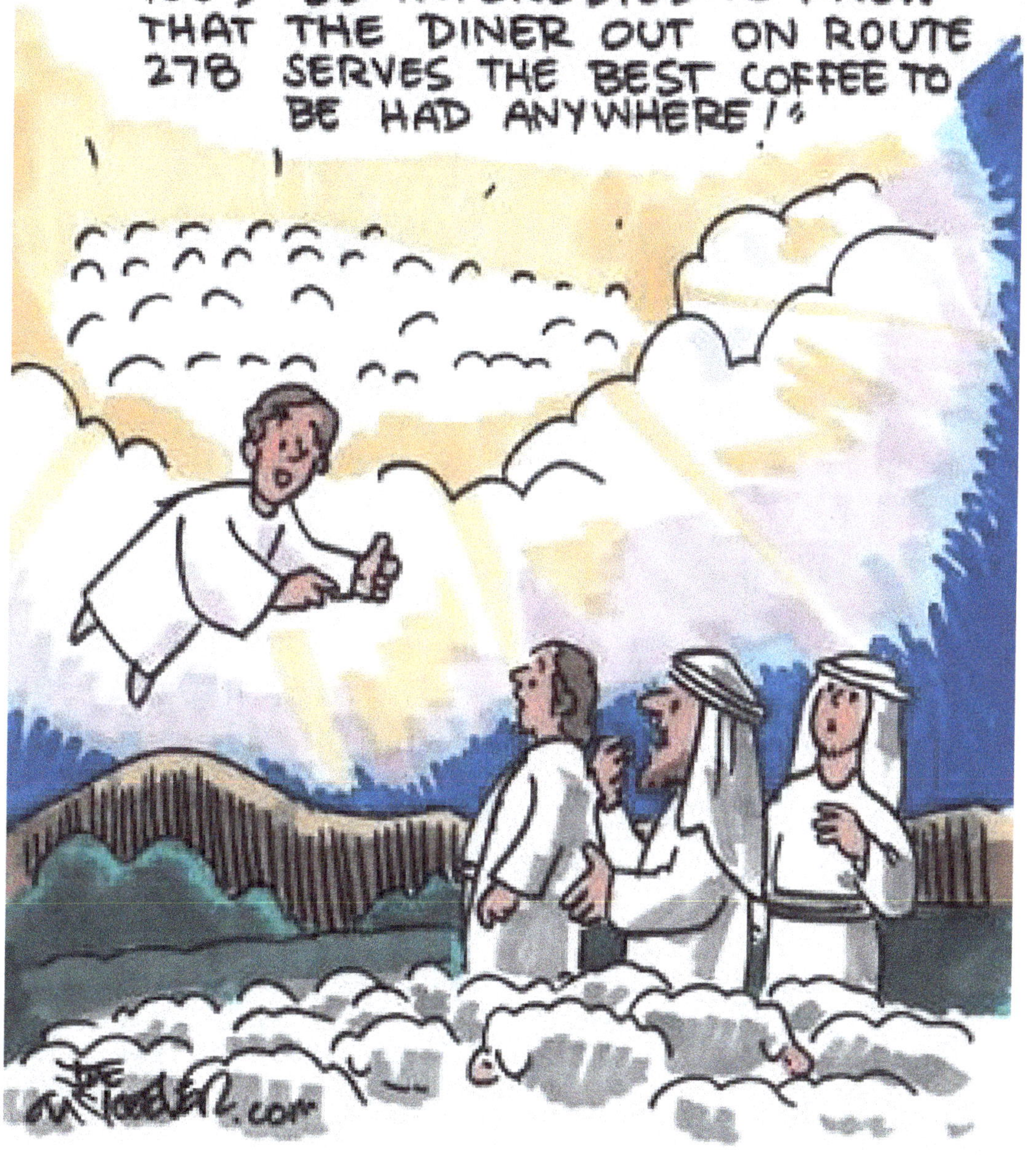

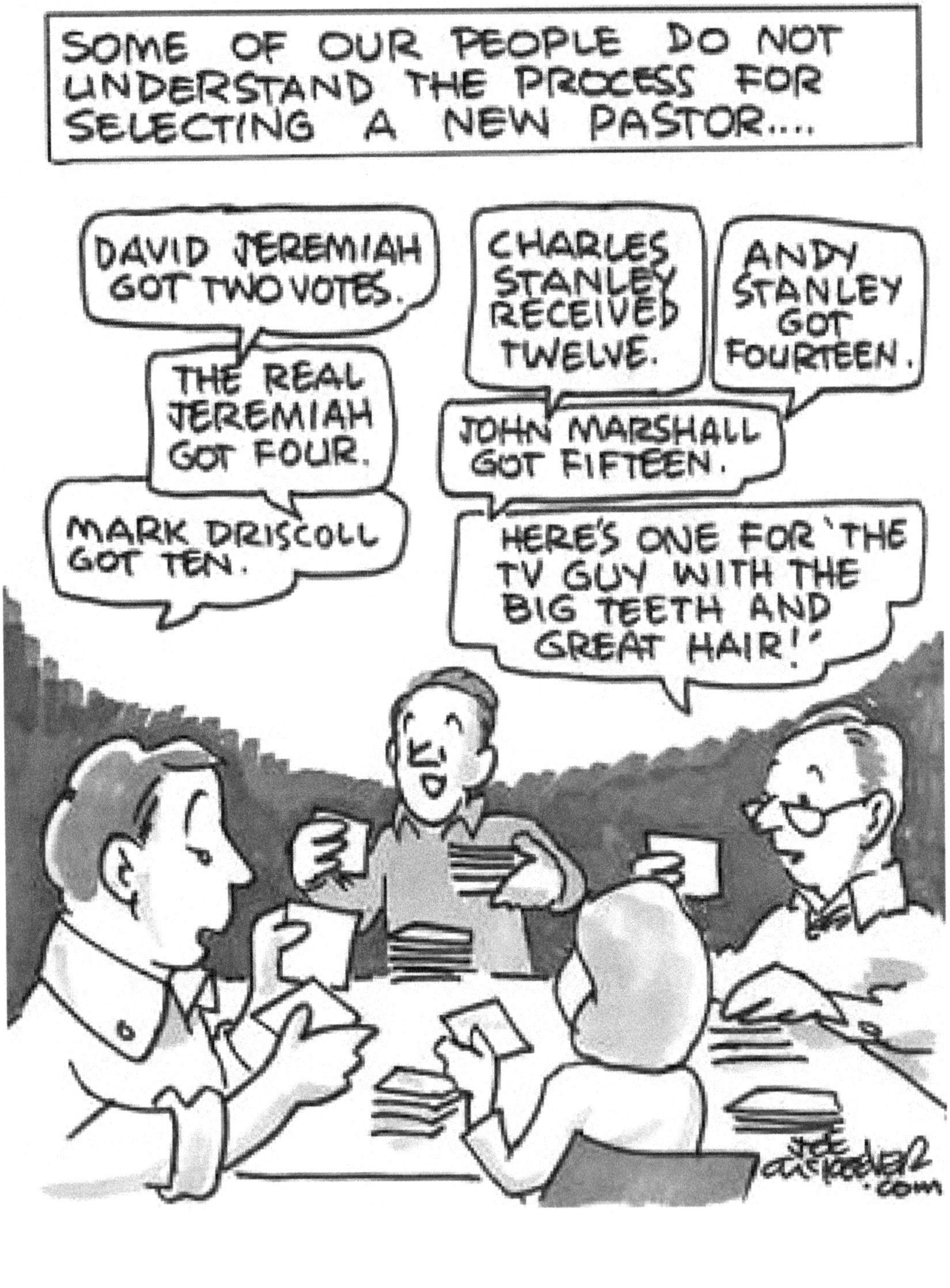
SOME OF OUR PEOPLE DO NOT UNDERSTAND THE PROCESS FOR SELECTING A NEW PASTOR....
DAVID JEREMIAH GOT TWO VOTES.
THE REAL JEREMIAH GOT FOUR.
MARK DRISCOLL GOT TEN.
CHARLES STANLEY RECEIVED TWELVE.
ANDY STANLEY GOT FOURTEEN.
JOHN MARSHALL GOT FIFTEEN.
HERE'S ONE FOR 'THE TV GUY WITH THE BIG TEETH AND GREAT HAIR!'

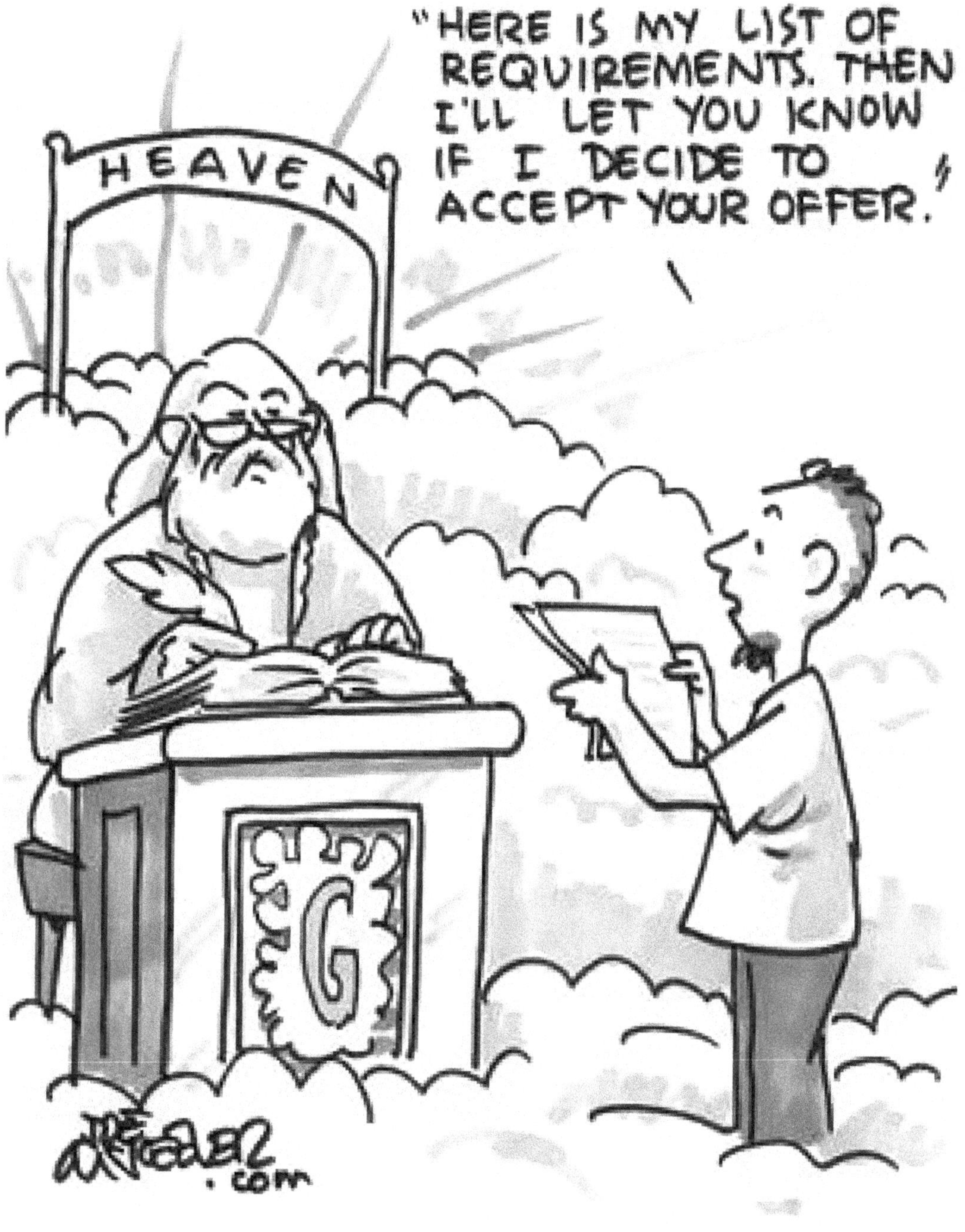
"HERE IS MY LIST OF REQUIREMENTS. THEN I'LL LET YOU KNOW IF I DECIDE TO ACCEPT YOUR OFFER."
HEAVEN

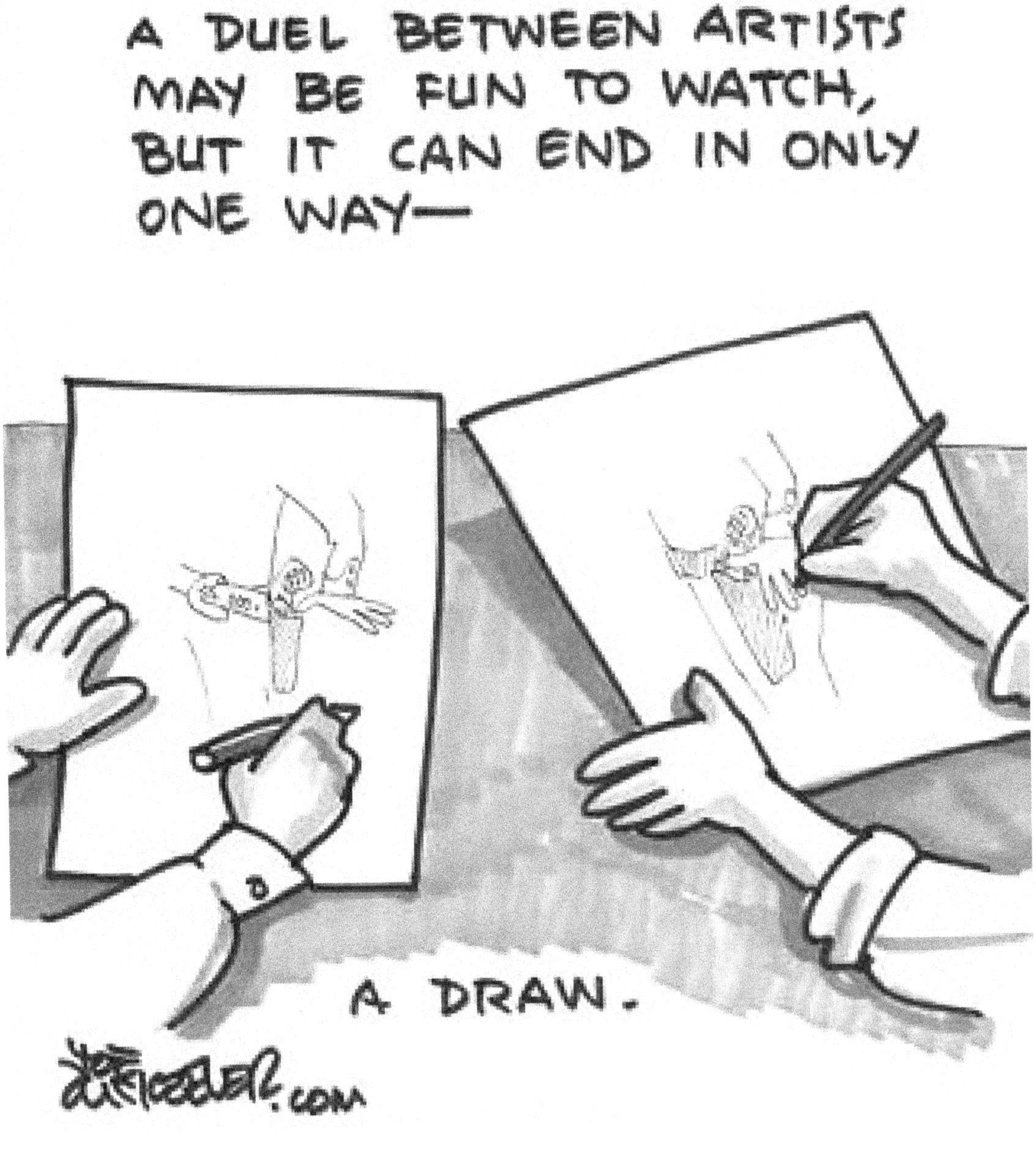
A DUEL BETWEEN ARTISTS MAY BE FUN TO WATCH, BUT IT CAN END IN ONLY ONE WAY—
A DRAW.

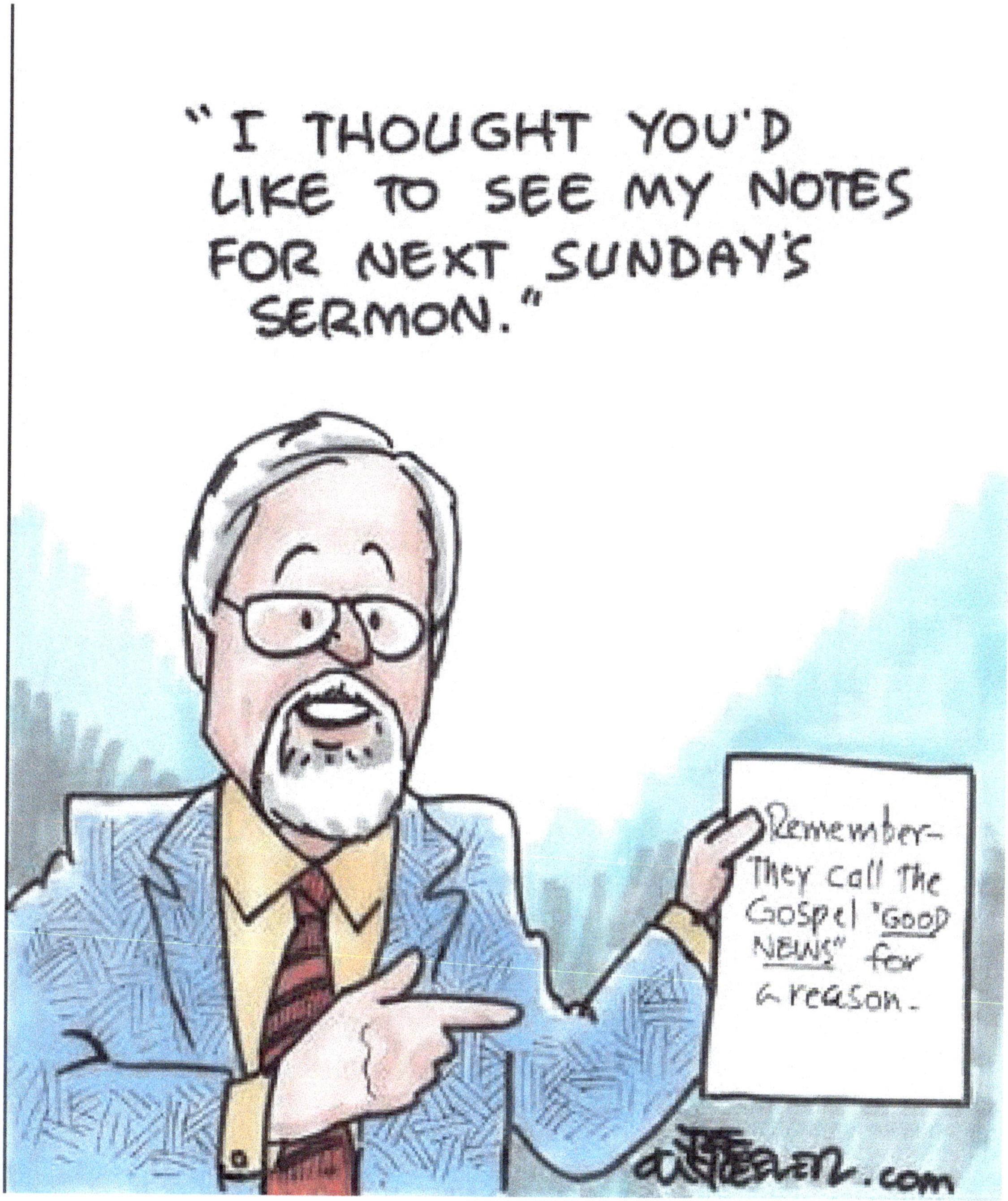
"I THOUGHT YOU'D LIKE TO SEE MY NOTES FOR NEXT SUNDAY'S SERMON."
Remember- They call the Gospel "GOOD NEWS" for a reason.

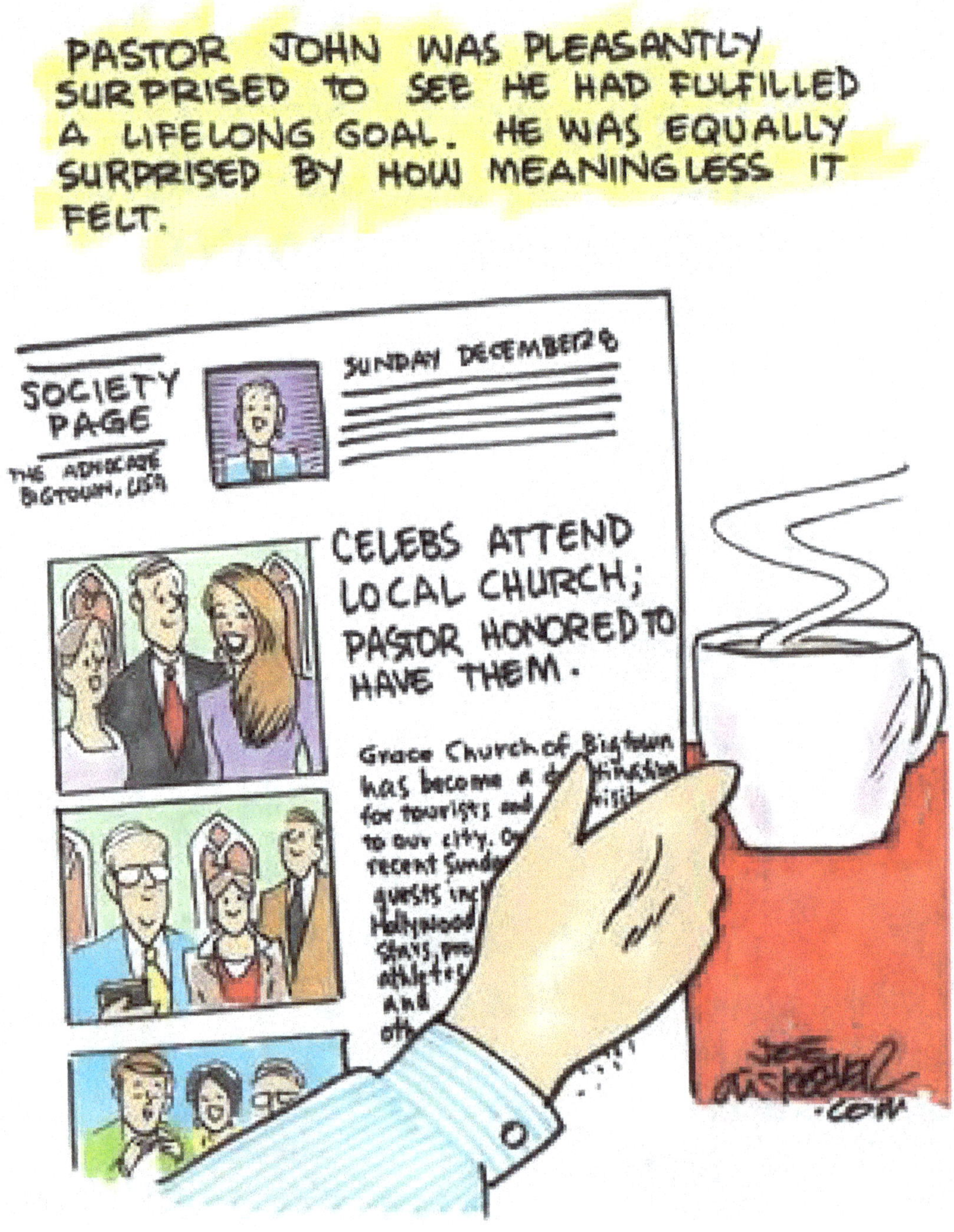
PASTOR JOHN WAS PLEASANTLY SURPRISED TO SEE HE HAD FULFILLED A LIFELONG GOAL. HE WAS EQUALLY SURPRISED BY HOW MEANINGLESS IT FELT.
SOCIETY PAGE
THE ADVOCATE
BIGTOWN, USA
SUNDAY DECEMBER 28
CELEBS ATTEND LOCAL CHURCH; PASTOR HONORED TO HAVE THEM.
Grace Church of Bigtown

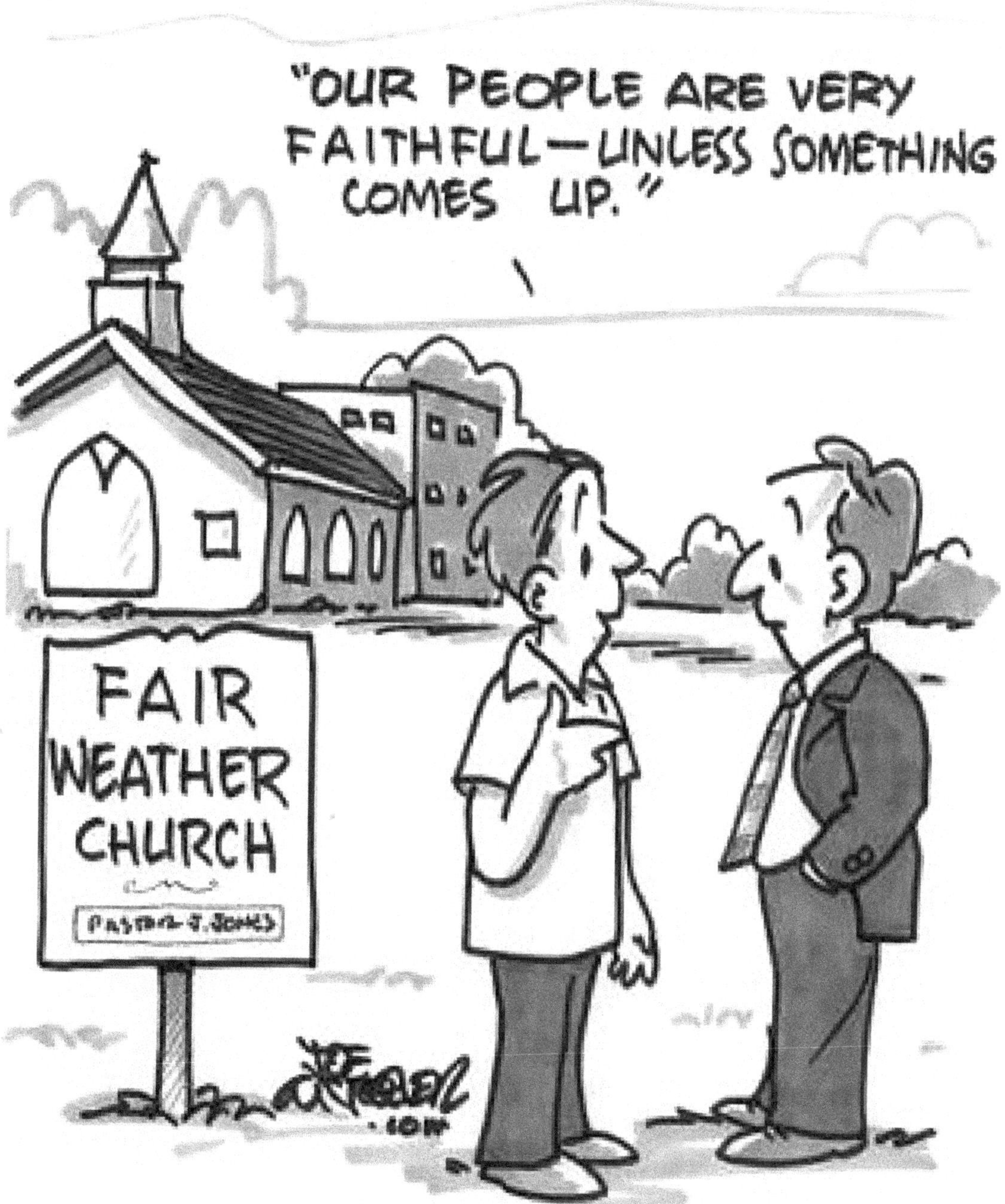
"OUR PEOPLE ARE VERY FAITHFUL—UNLESS SOMETHING COMES UP."
FAIR WEATHER CHURCH

SHOOTING THE HOLIDAY PHOTO

"THAT BIBLE IN YOUR HAND WOULD BE MORE IMPRESSIVE IF YOU HADN'T HAD TO BORROW IT FROM THE NEIGHBORS!"

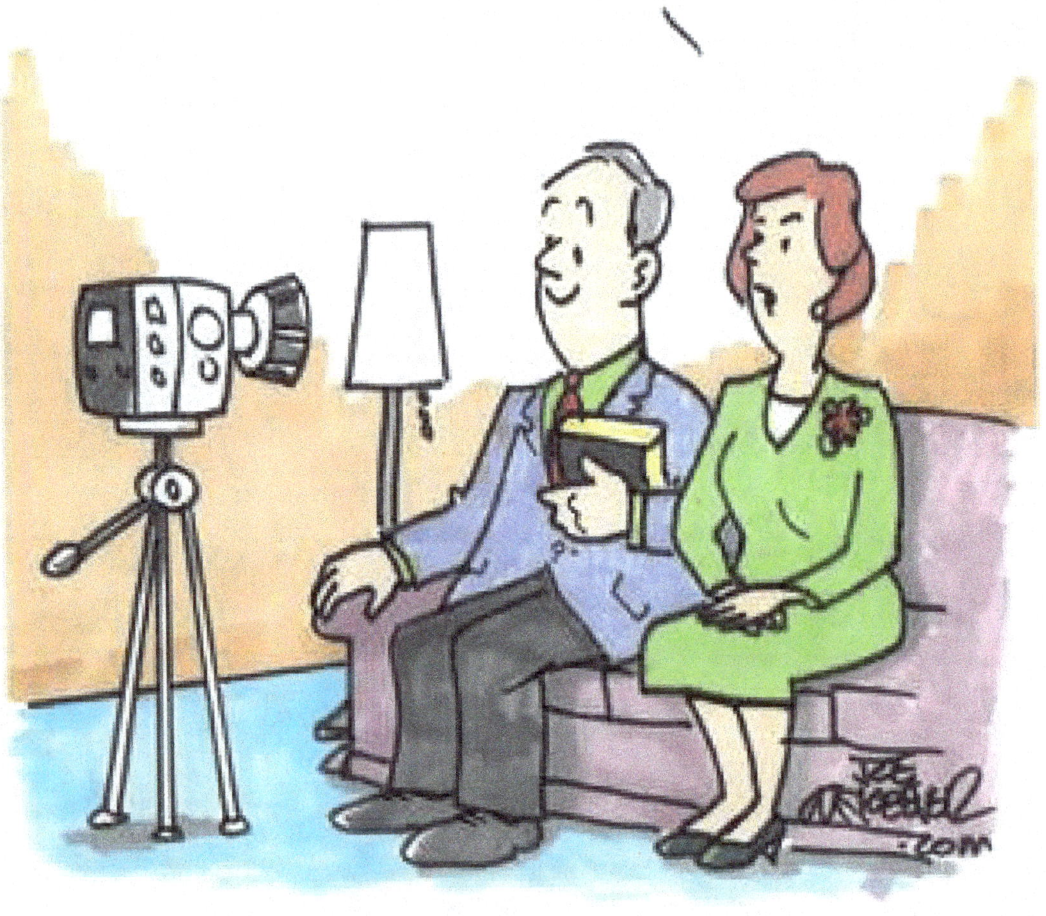

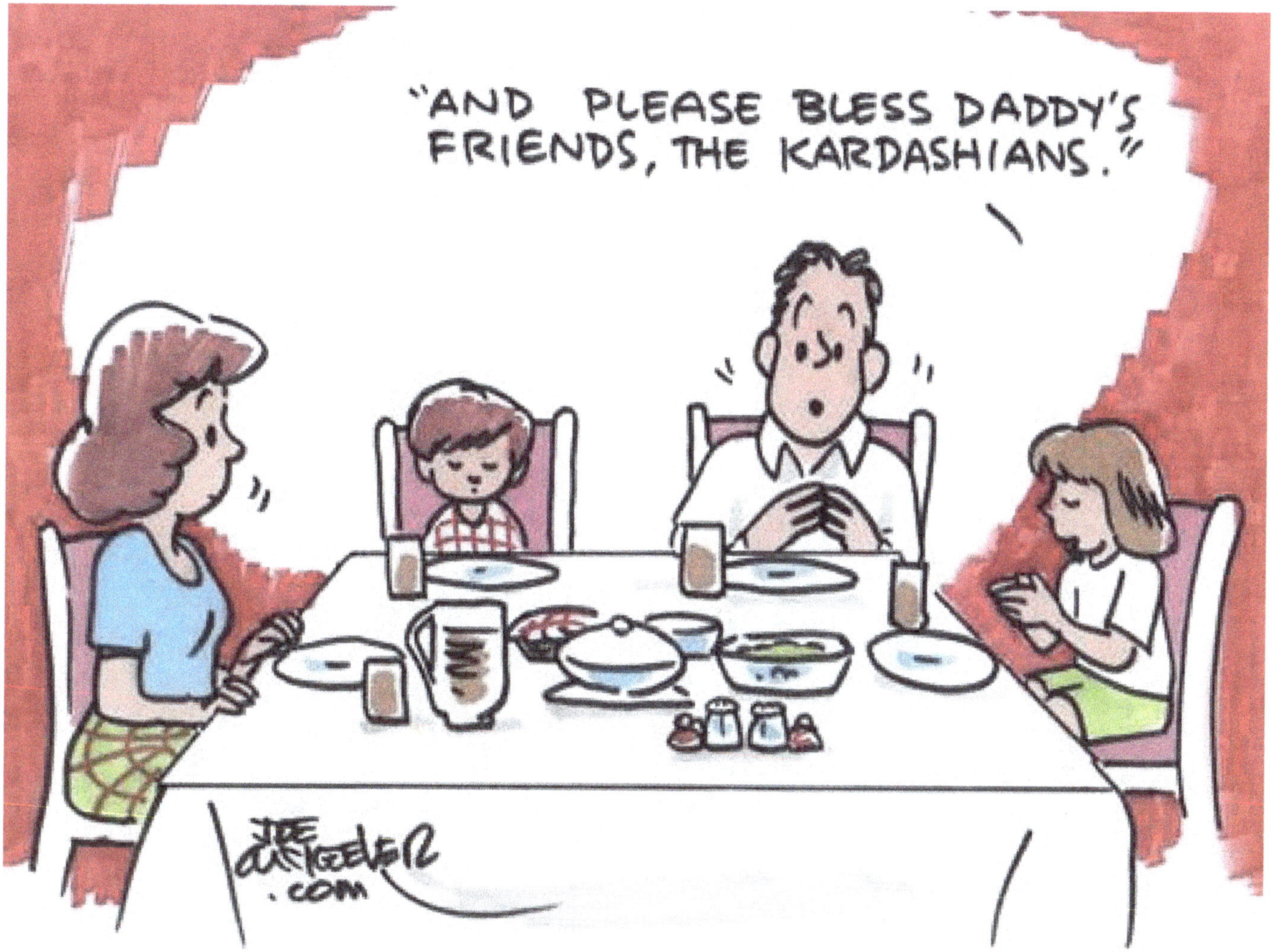
"AND PLEASE BLESS DADDY'S FRIENDS, THE KARDASHIANS."

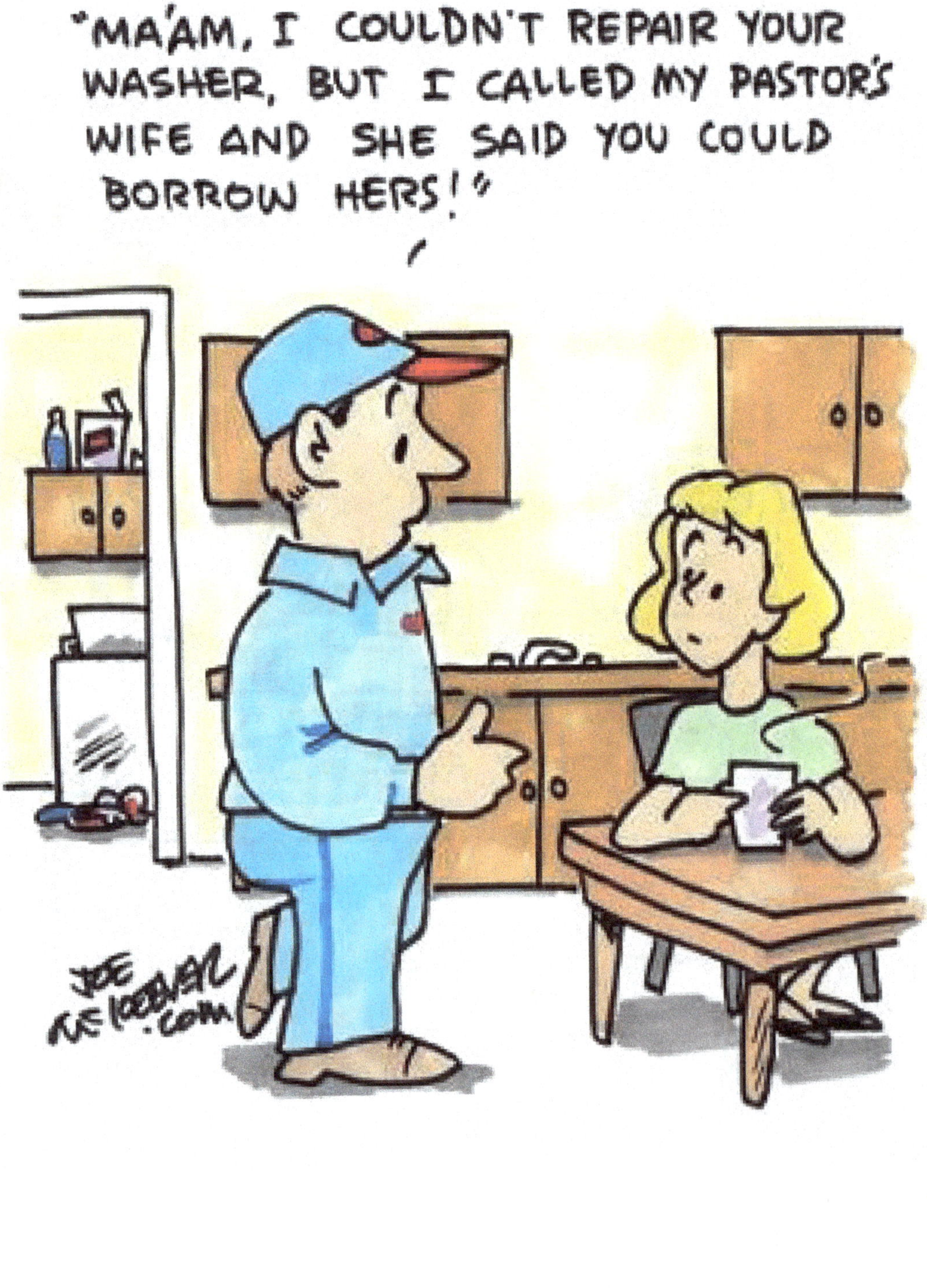
"MA'AM, I COULDN'T REPAIR YOUR WASHER, BUT I CALLED MY PASTOR'S WIFE AND SHE SAID YOU COULD BORROW HERS!"
JOE MCKEEVER .com

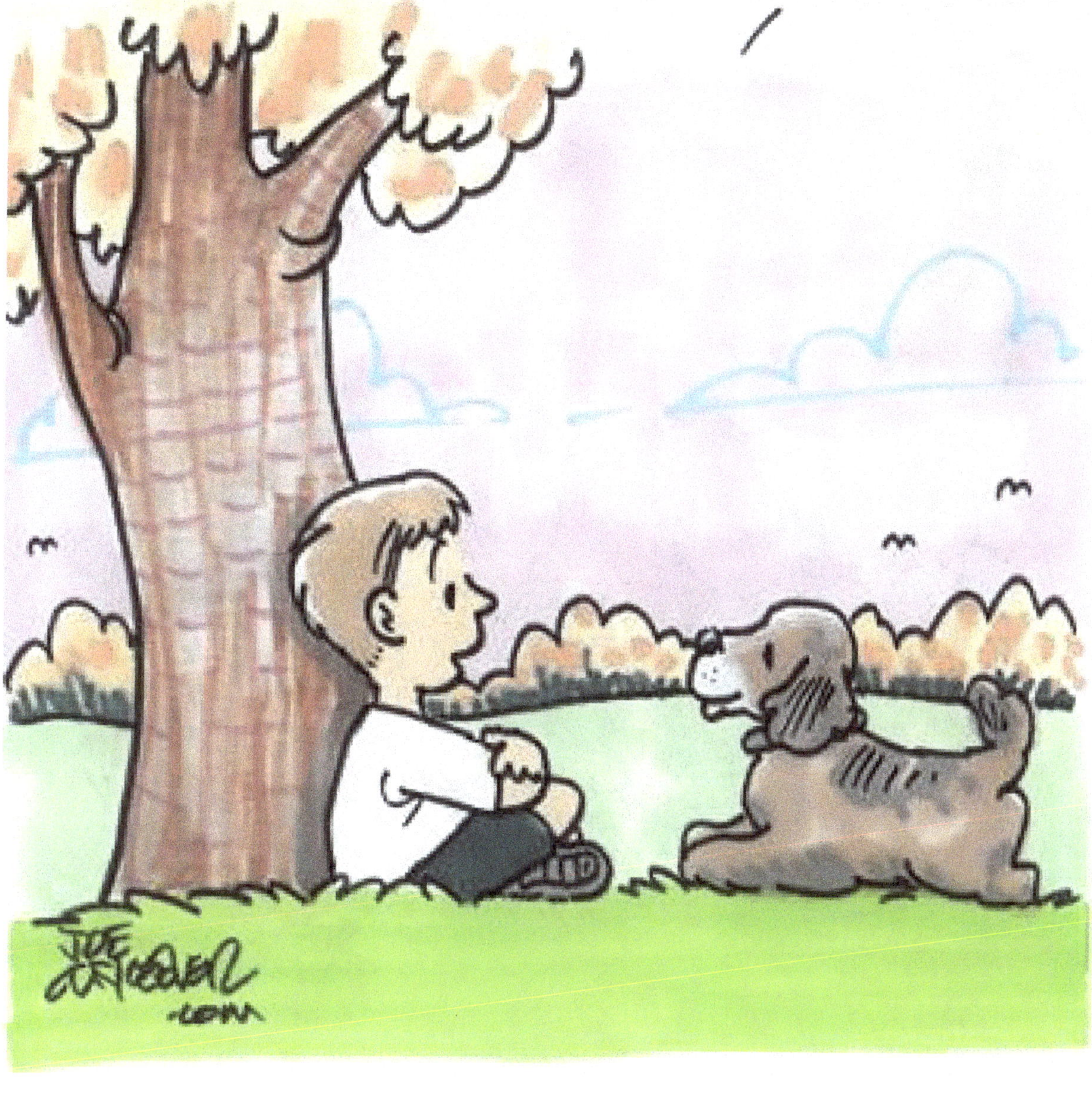

"OF COURSE WE WERE CREATED BY THE SAME GOD. HOW ELSE DO YOU EXPLAIN US BEING SO SMART AND NICE?"

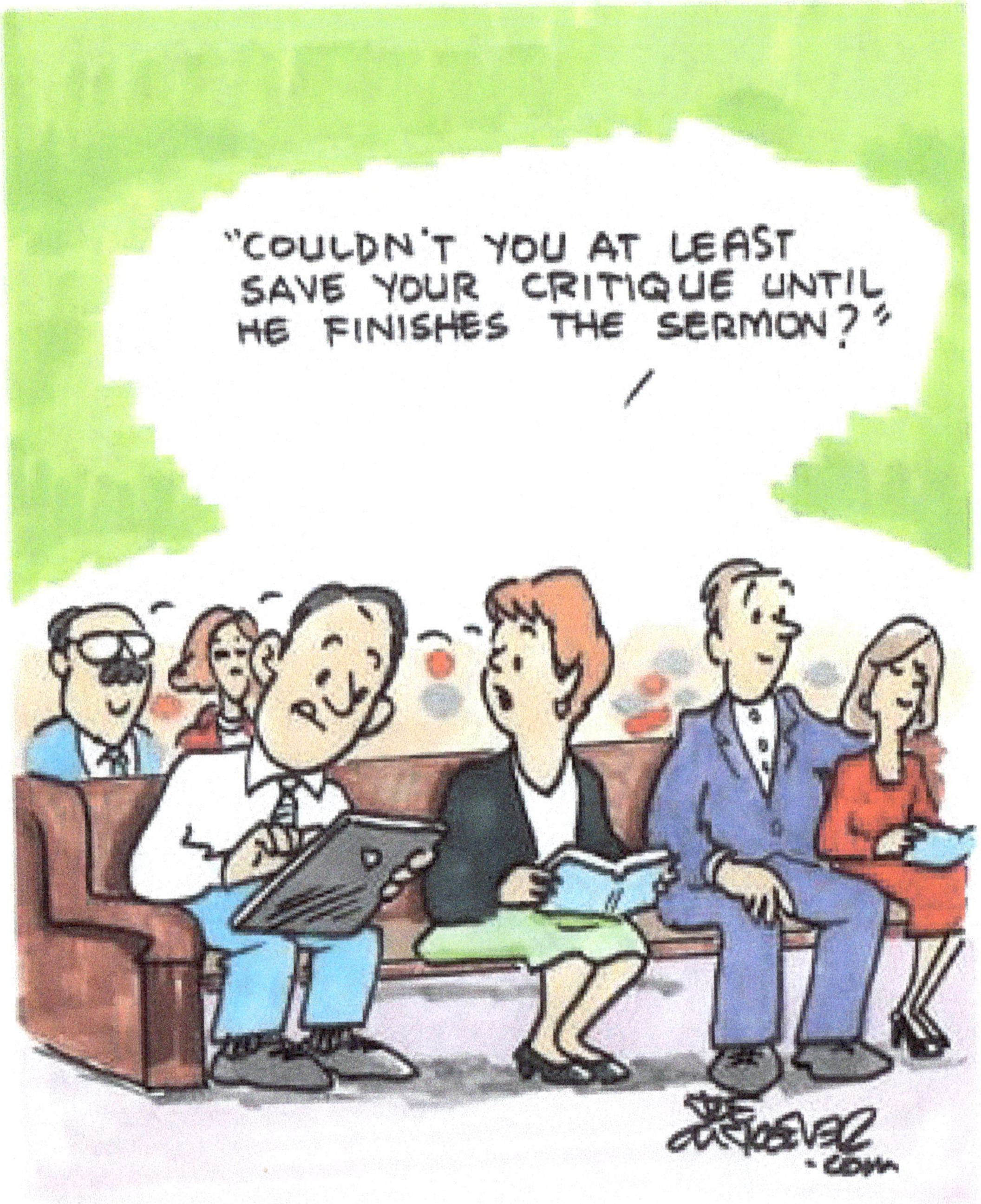
"COULDN'T YOU AT LEAST SAVE YOUR CRITIQUE UNTIL HE FINISHES THE SERMON?"

"YES SIR, I TRY TO WORK IN A SPORTS STORY IN ALL MY SERMONS— WHETHER IT FITS OR NOT!"

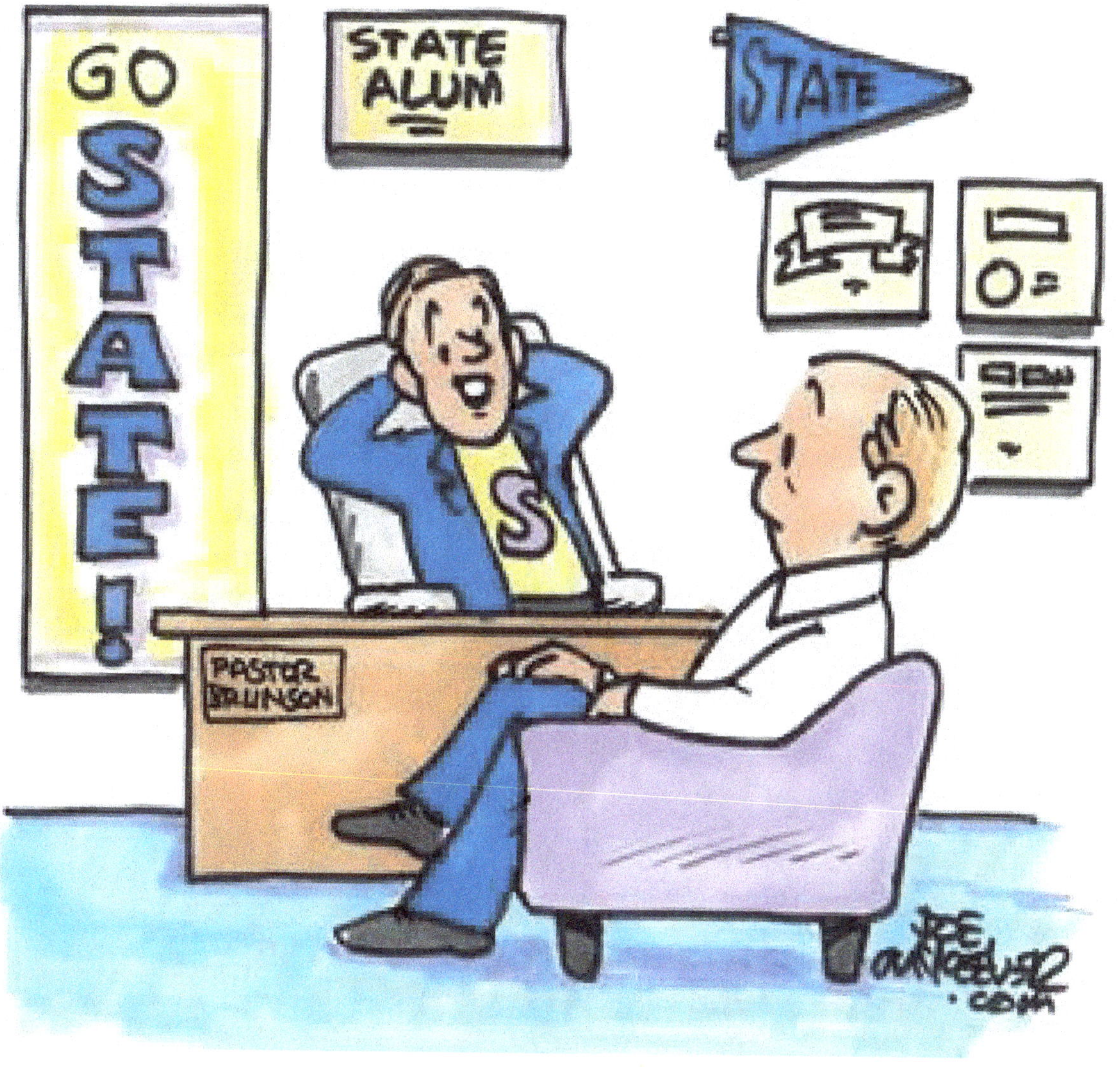
GO STATE!
STATE ALUM
STATE
PASTOR

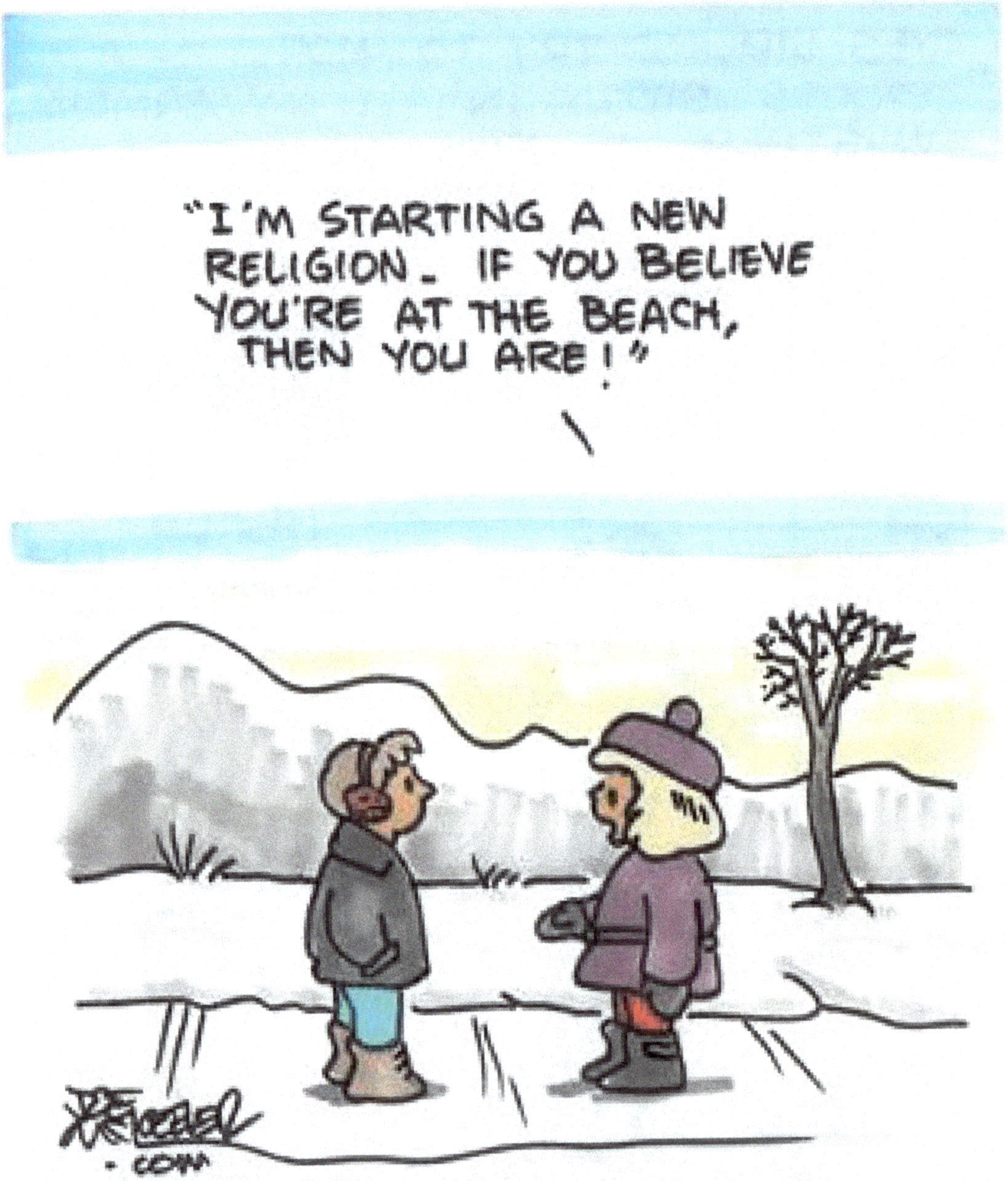
"I'M STARTING A NEW RELIGION. IF YOU BELIEVE YOU'RE AT THE BEACH, THEN YOU ARE!"

(HONEY, THAT RELIGION IS OLDER THAN YOUR GREAT-GRANDPA!)

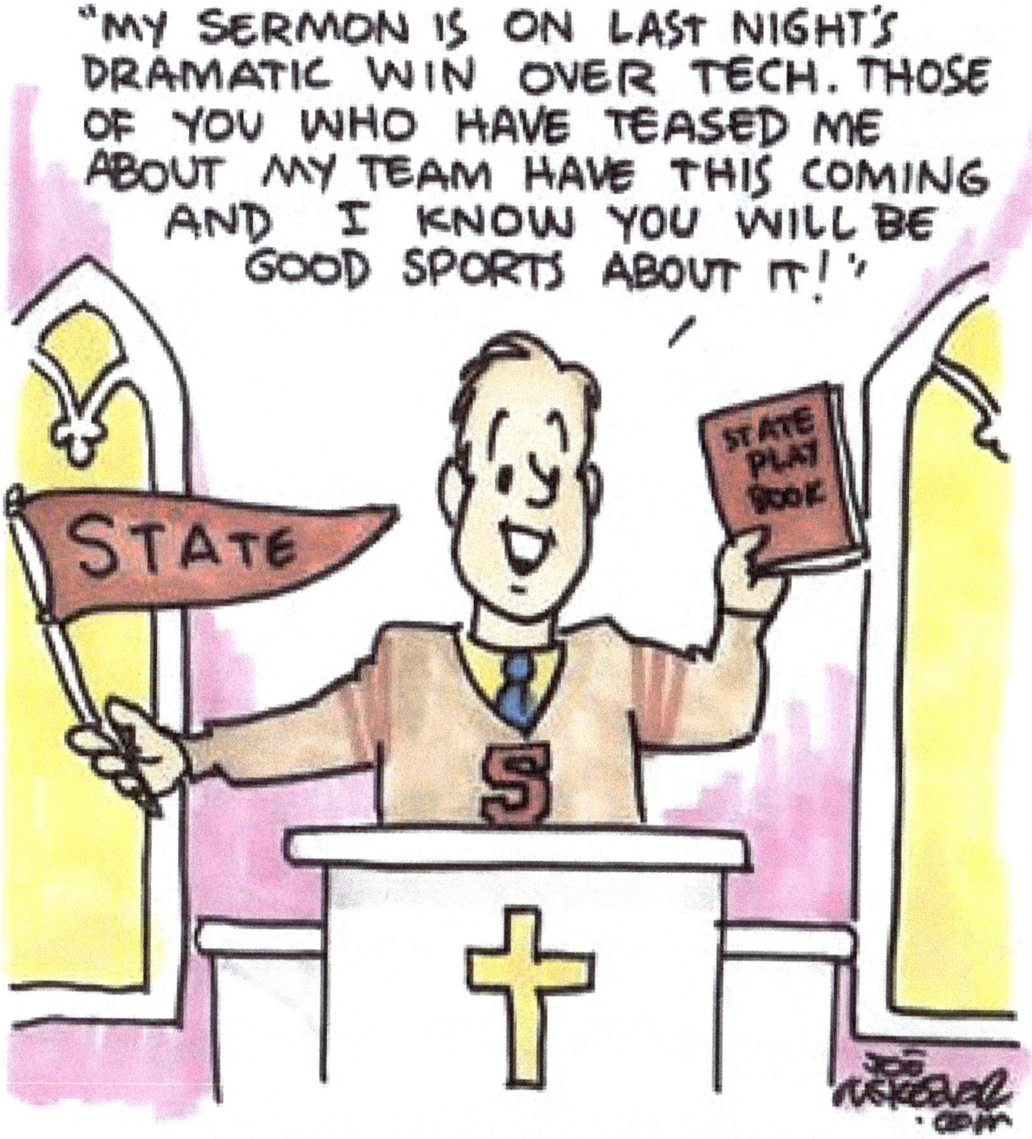
"MY SERMON IS ON LAST NIGHT'S DRAMATIC WIN OVER TECH. THOSE OF YOU WHO HAVE TEASED ME ABOUT MY TEAM HAVE THIS COMING AND I KNOW YOU WILL BE GOOD SPORTS ABOUT IT!"
STATE
STATE PLAY BOOK
S

JUST BEFORE HE WAS FIRED.

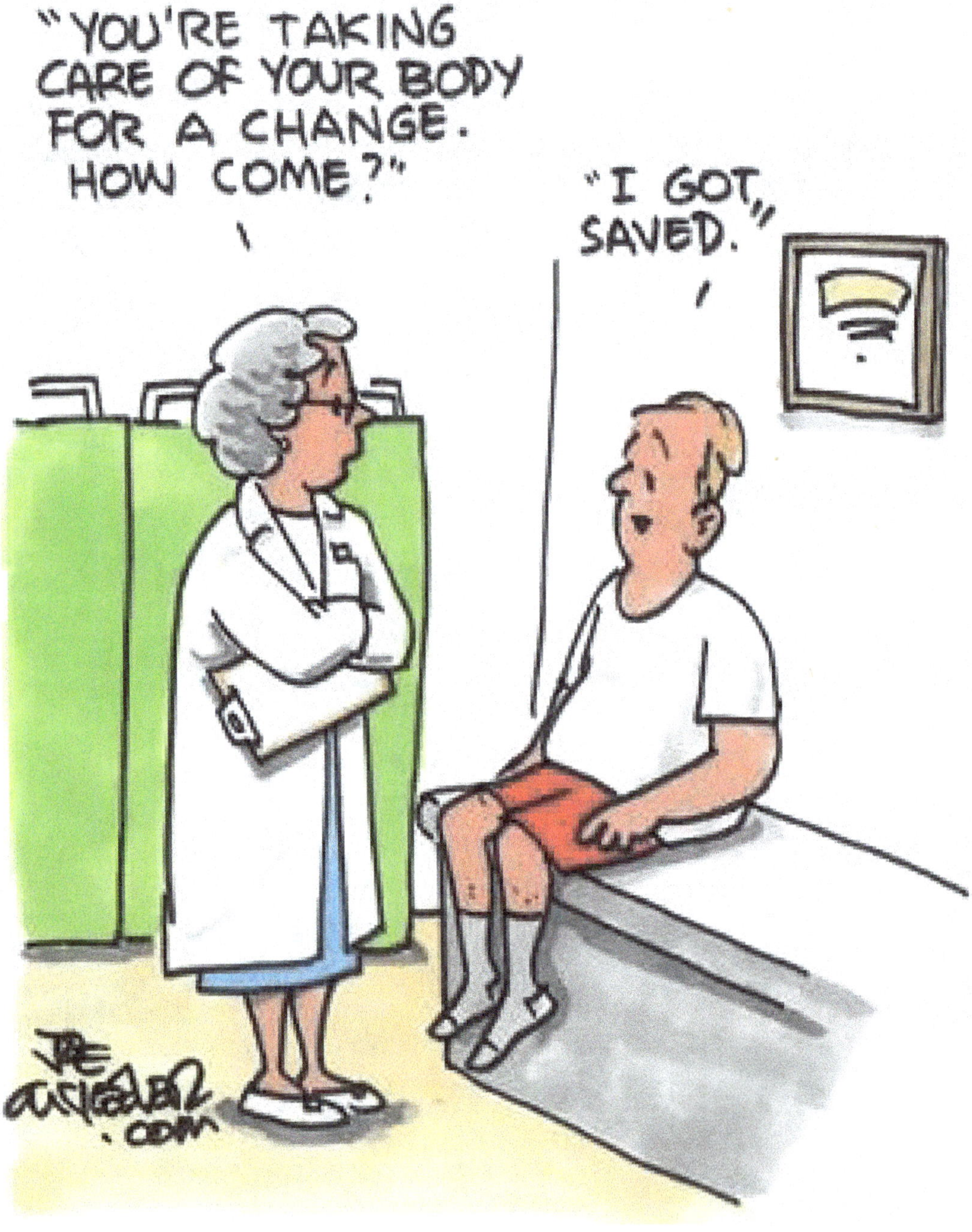
"YOU'RE TAKING CARE OF YOUR BODY FOR A CHANGE. HOW COME?"
"I GOT SAVED."
JOE CARTOONIST? .COM

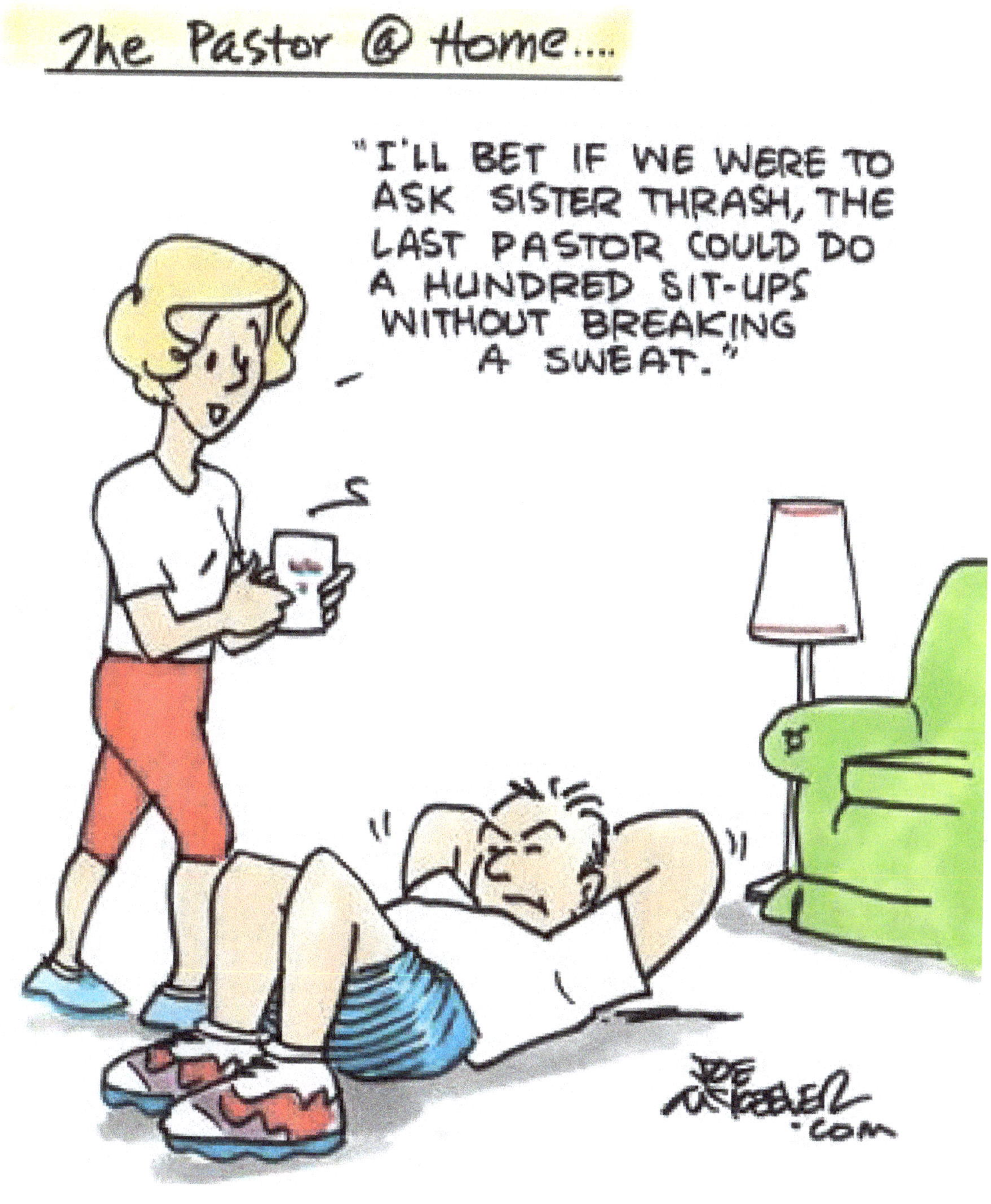
The Pastor @ Home....
"I'LL BET IF WE WERE TO ASK SISTER THRASH, THE LAST PASTOR COULD DO A HUNDRED SIT-UPS WITHOUT BREAKING A SWEAT."

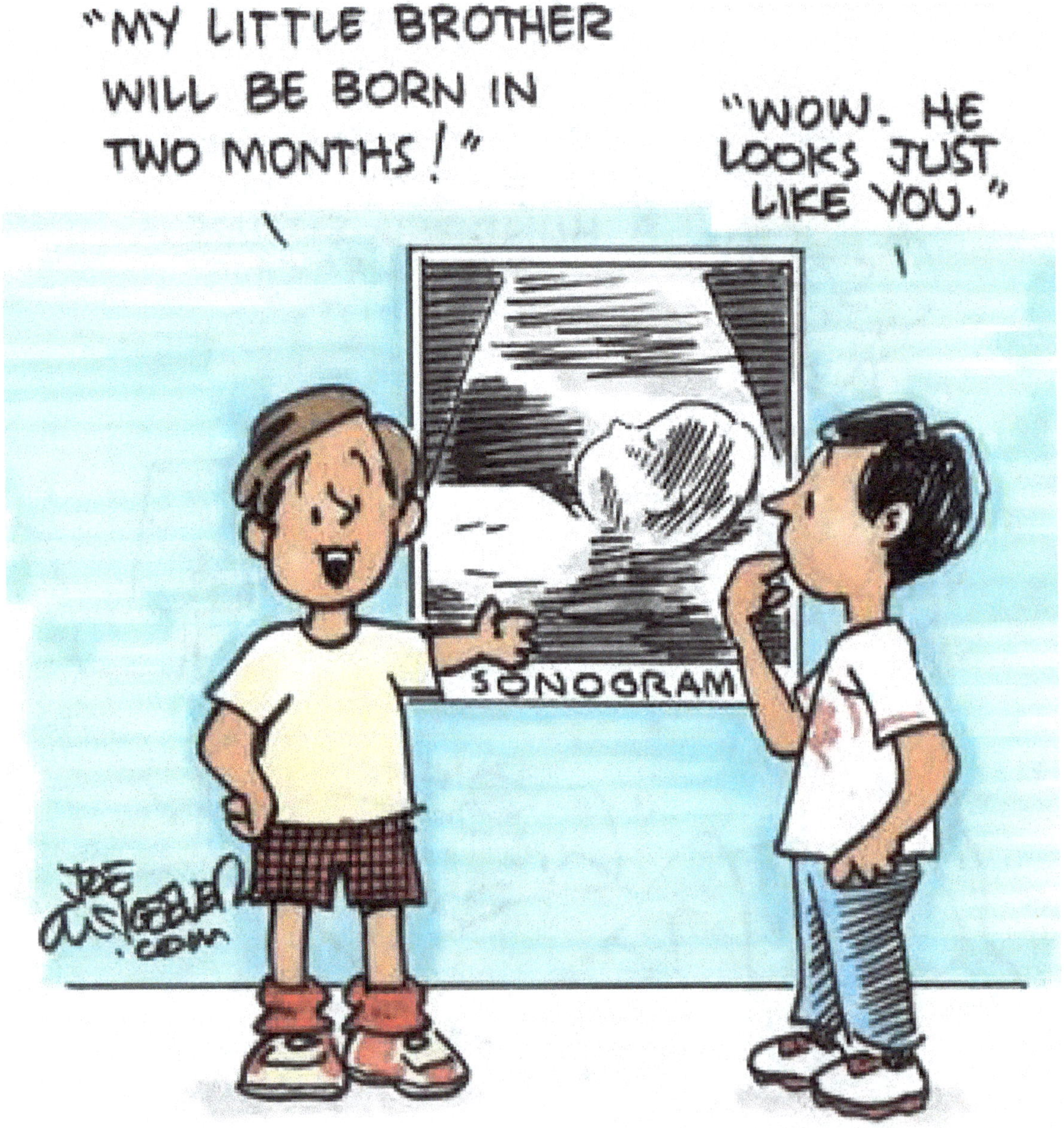
"MY LITTLE BROTHER WILL BE BORN IN TWO MONTHS!"
SONOGRAM
"WOW. HE LOOKS JUST LIKE YOU."

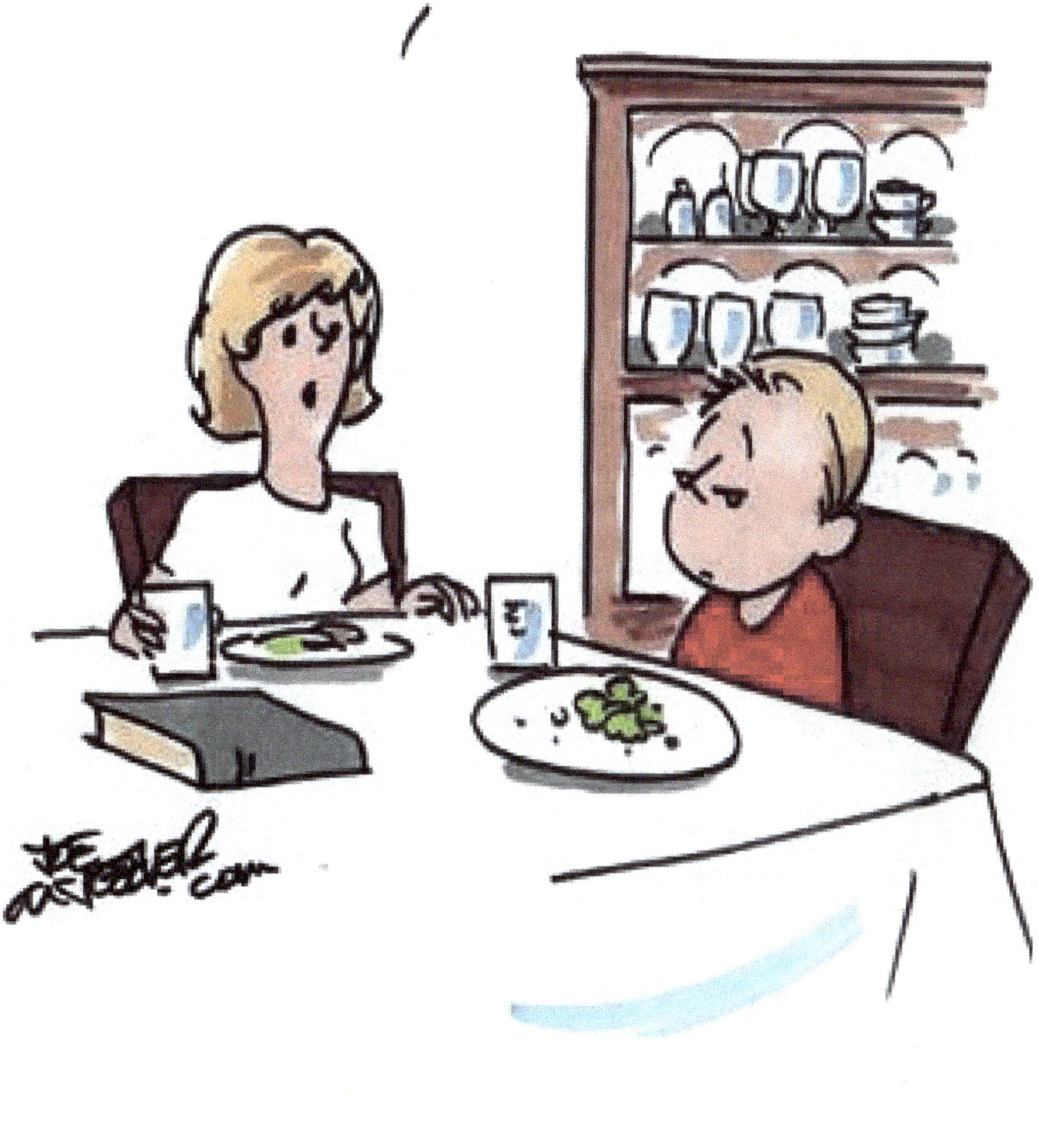

"EAT YOUR BROCCOLI, BILLY—OR NO SECOND TIMOTHY FOR YOU TONIGHT!"

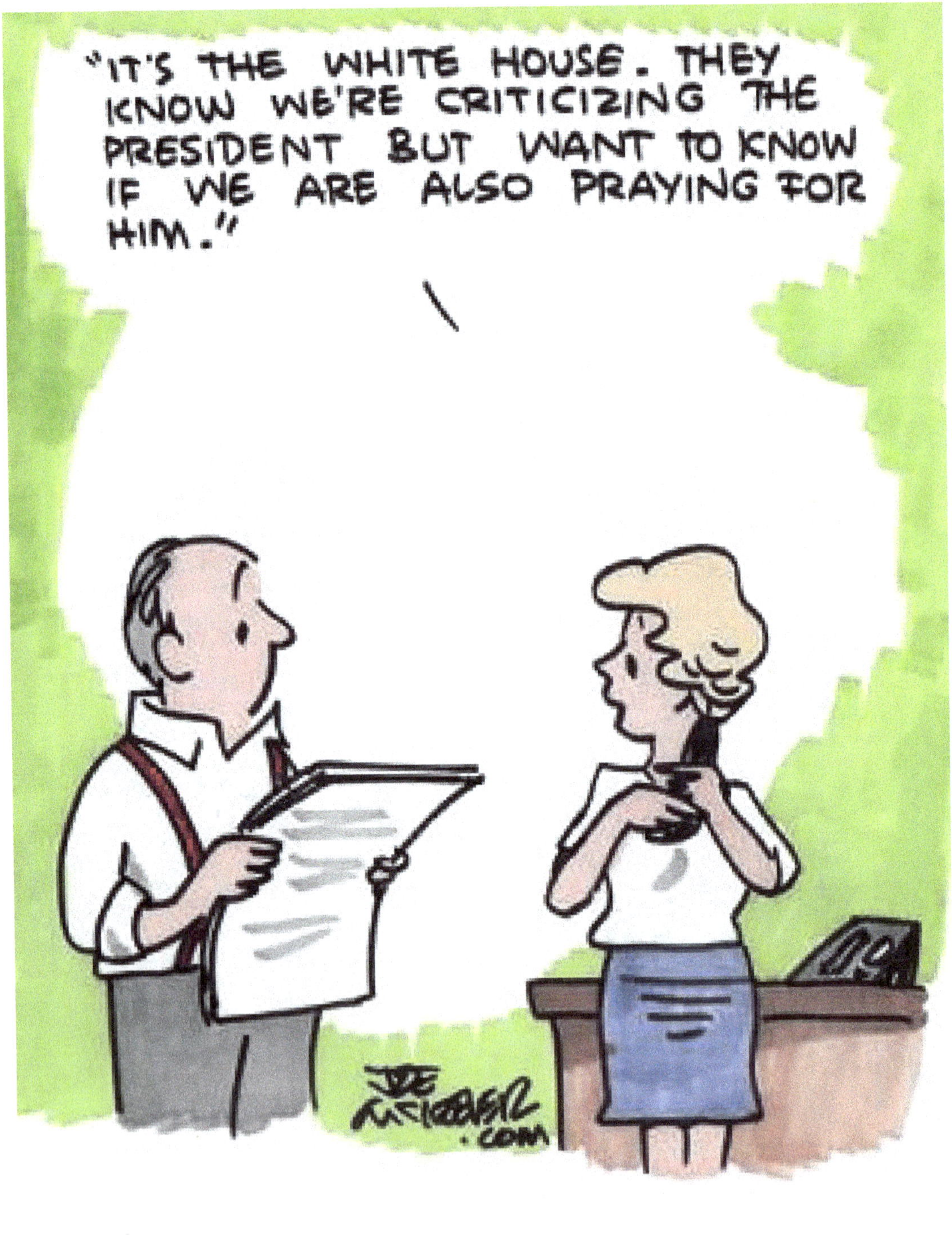
"IT'S THE WHITE HOUSE. THEY KNOW WE'RE CRITICIZING THE PRESIDENT BUT WANT TO KNOW IF WE ARE ALSO PRAYING FOR HIM."
JOE McKEEVER .COM

"THE PASTOR SAYS I WON THE CHURCH LOTTERY AND GET TO GIVE MY TITHE FOR THE NEXT YEAR. I'M SO BLESSED- THIS IS THE THIRD YEAR IN A ROW I'VE WON!"

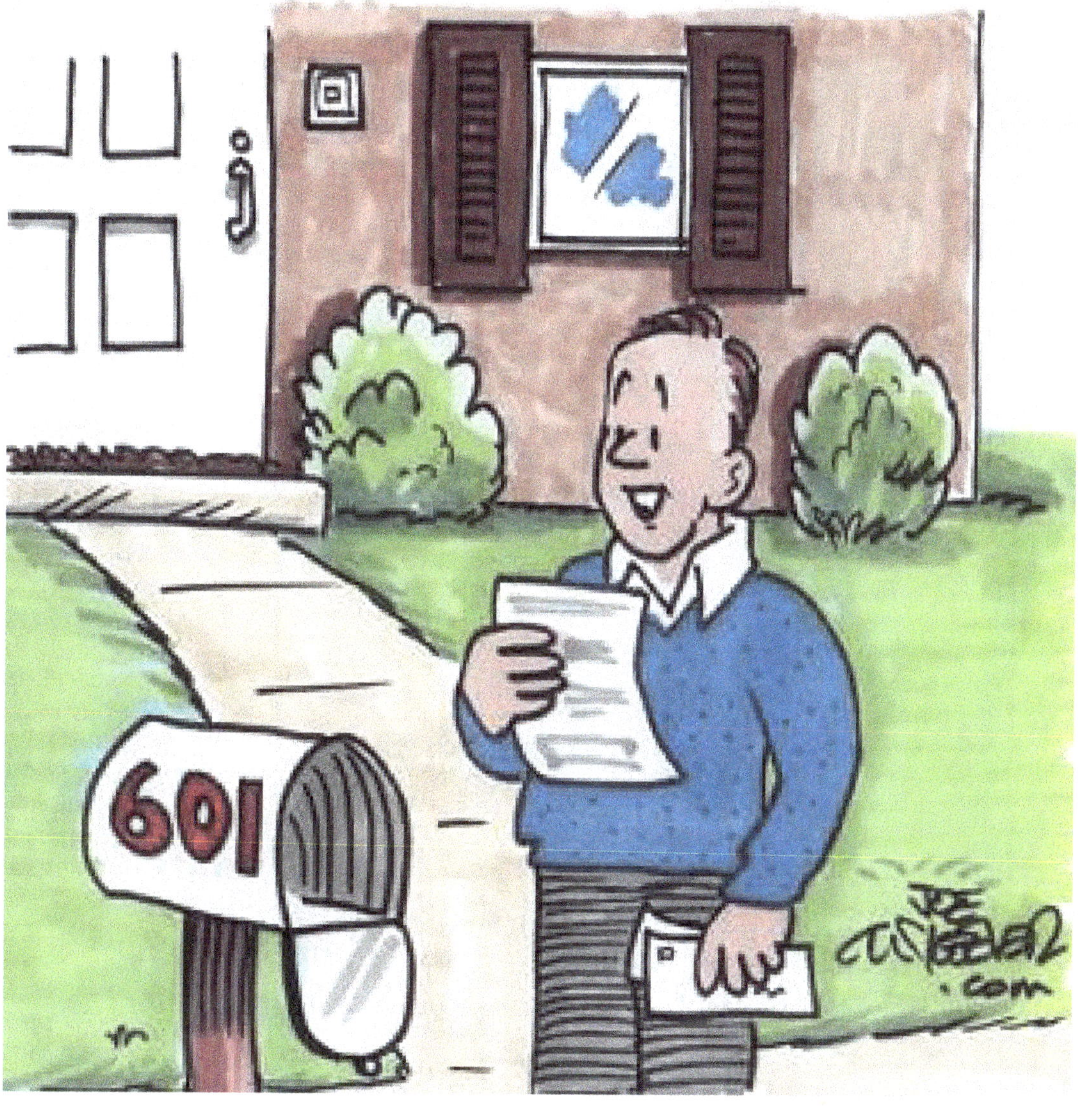
601

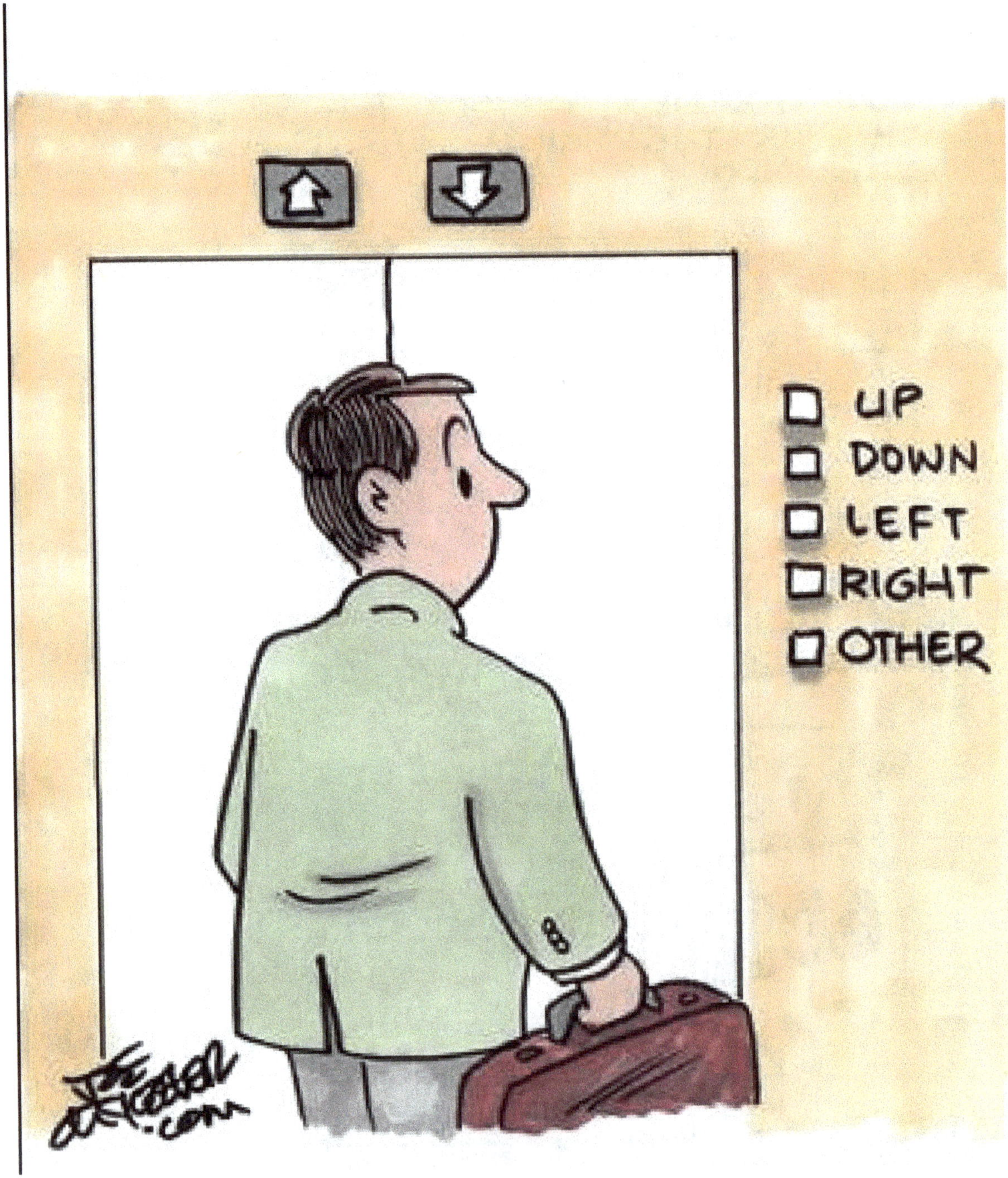
UP
DOWN
LEFT
RIGHT
OTHER

"C'MON, GUYS—THERE HAS TO BE A BETTER WAY TO SETTLE THE CALVINISM THING!"

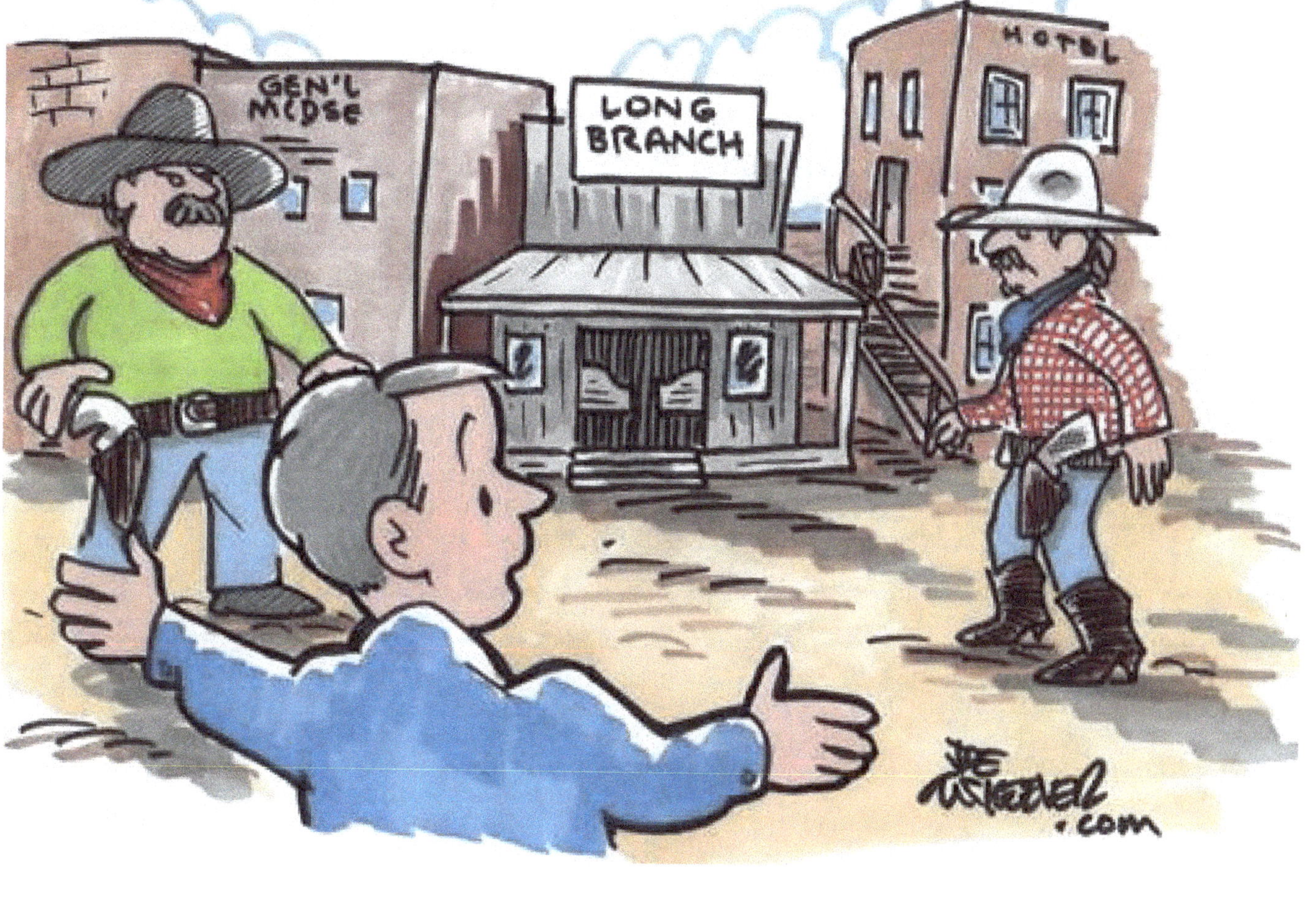
GEN'L MCDSE
LONG BRANCH
HOTEL

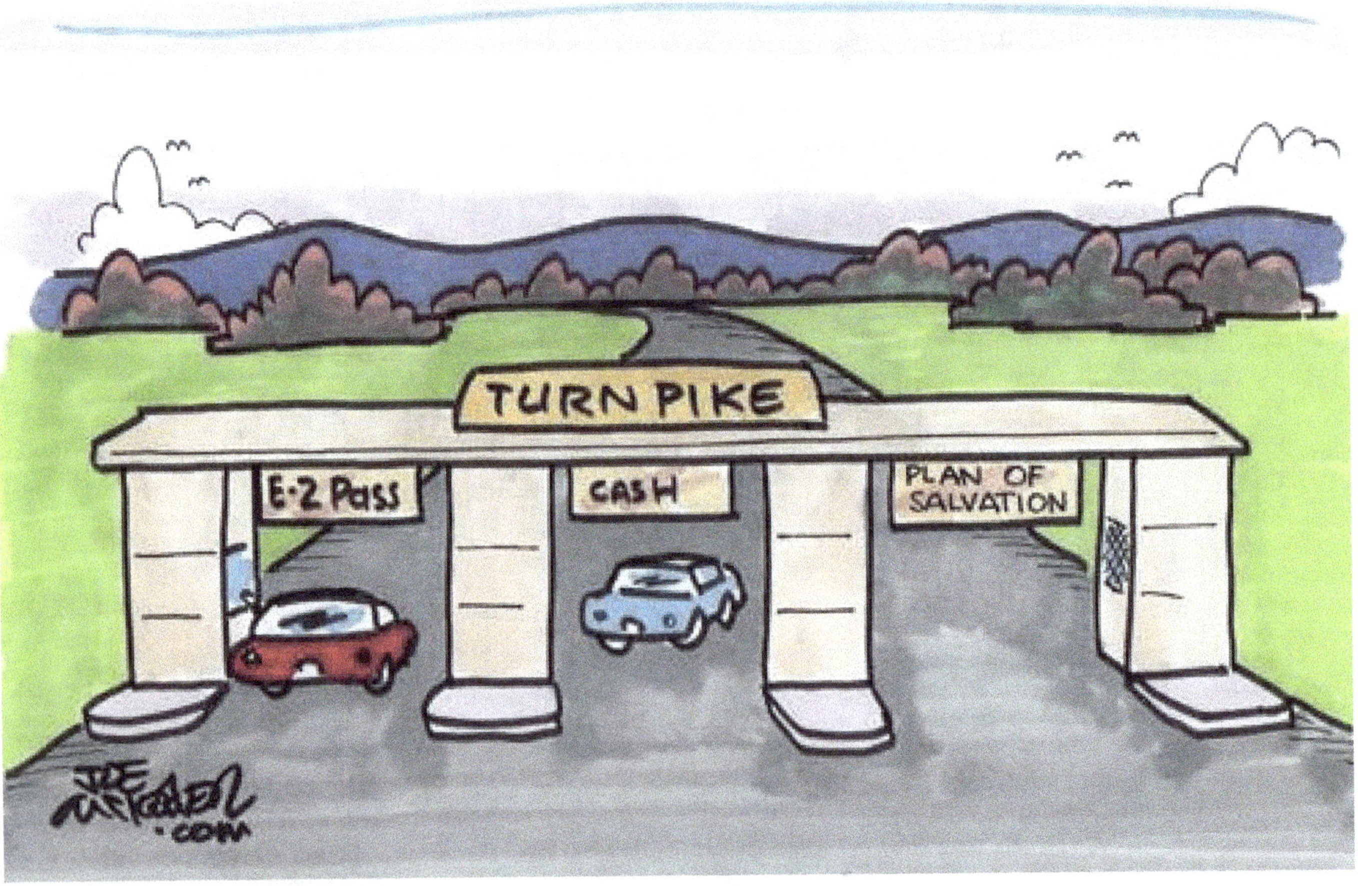
TURN PIKE
E-Z Pass
CASH
PLAN OF SALVATION

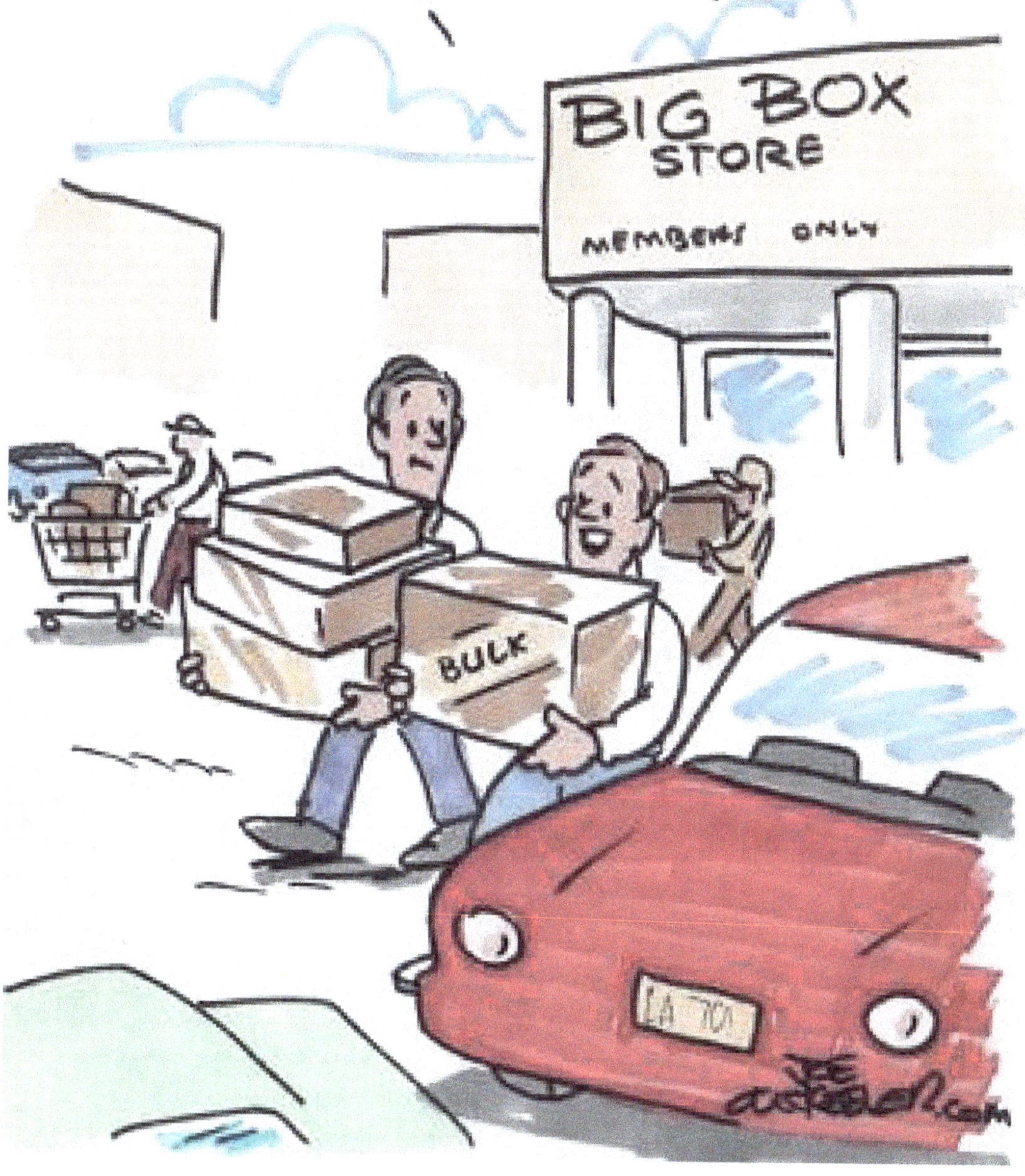
BIG BOX
STORE
MEMBERS ONLY
BULK
LA 701

"GOOD THING I DON'T ACTUALLY NEED THIS STUFF, BECAUSE I DON'T HAVE ANYWHERE TO STORE IT!"

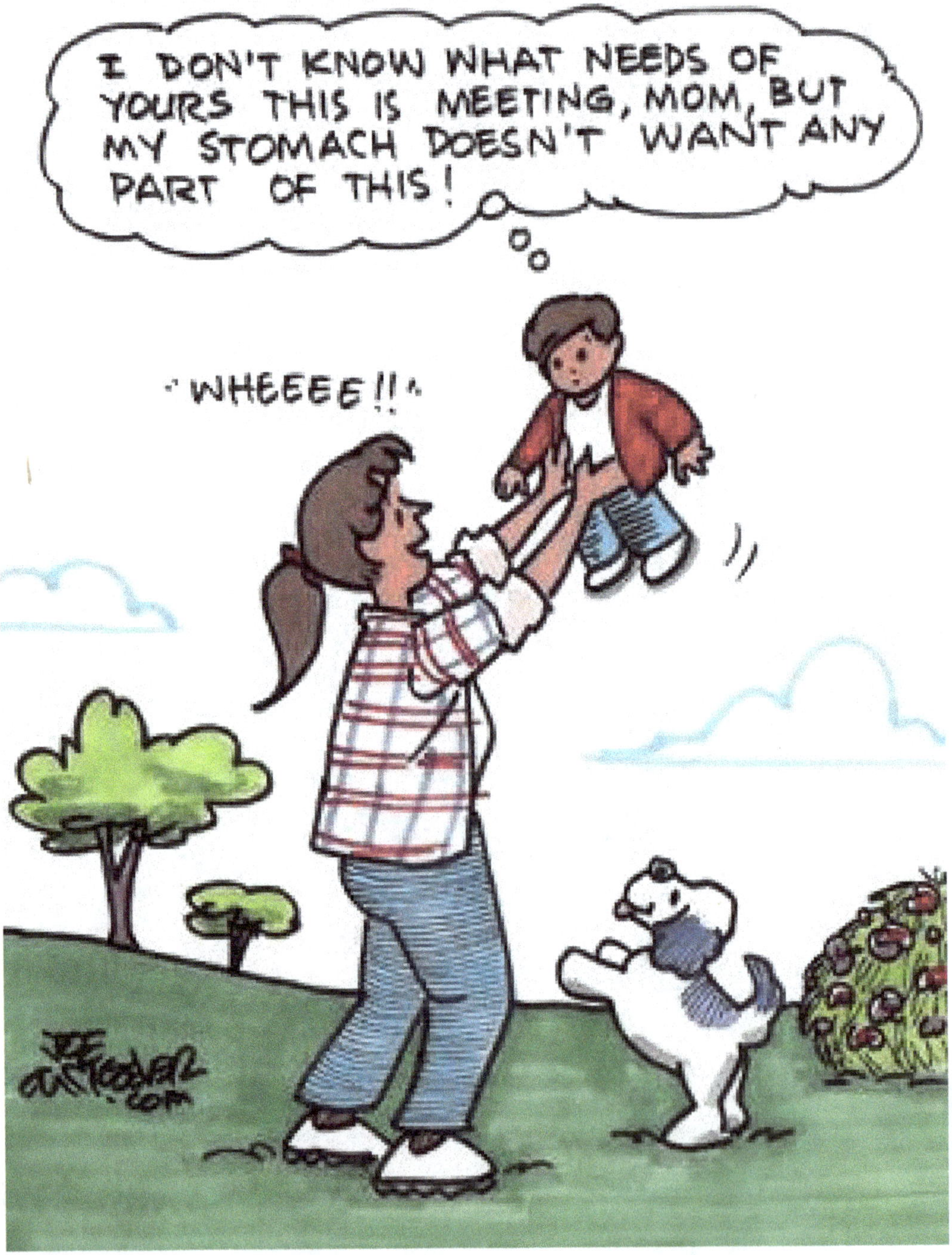
I DON'T KNOW WHAT NEEDS OF YOURS THIS IS MEETING, MOM, BUT MY STOMACH DOESN'T WANT ANY PART OF THIS!
"WHEEEEE!!"

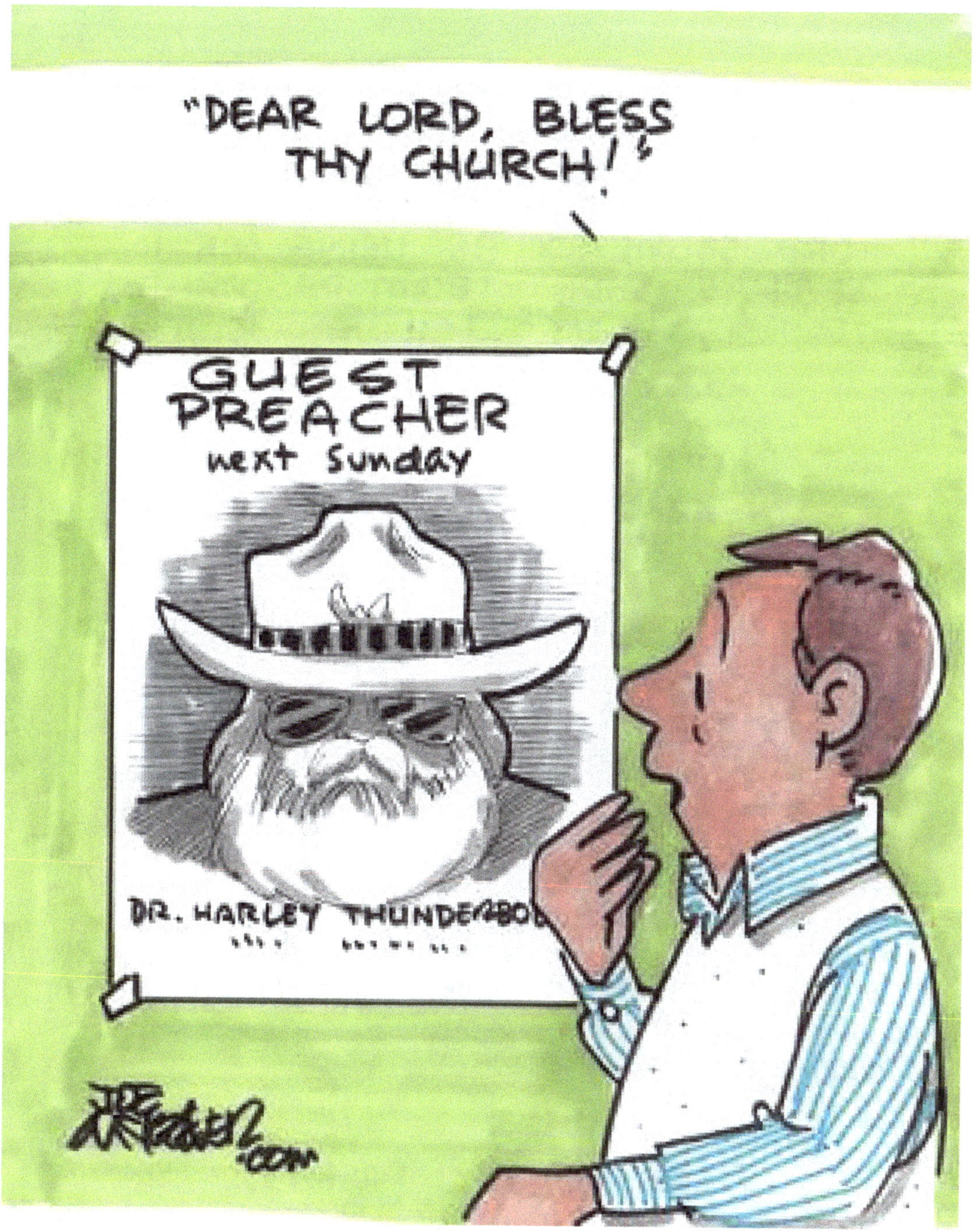
"DEAR LORD, BLESS THY CHURCH!"
GUEST PREACHER
next Sunday
DR. HARLEY THUNDERBO

"HONEY, WHICH SOUNDS BETTER ON MY RESUME—'I WAS FIRED FROM MY LAST TWO CHURCHES AFTER LESS THAN A YEAR IN EACH' OR 'THE LORD SEEMS TO BE USING ME IN SEVERAL SHORT-TERM PASTORATES'?"

Pray for our pastors!

"I KNOW I ONLY STARTED AS YOUR YOUTH MINISTER YESTERDAY, PASTOR — BUT AFTER MEETING THE KIDS LAST NIGHT, I'D LIKE AN ASSISTANT, HEALTH INSURANCE, AND A RAISE!"

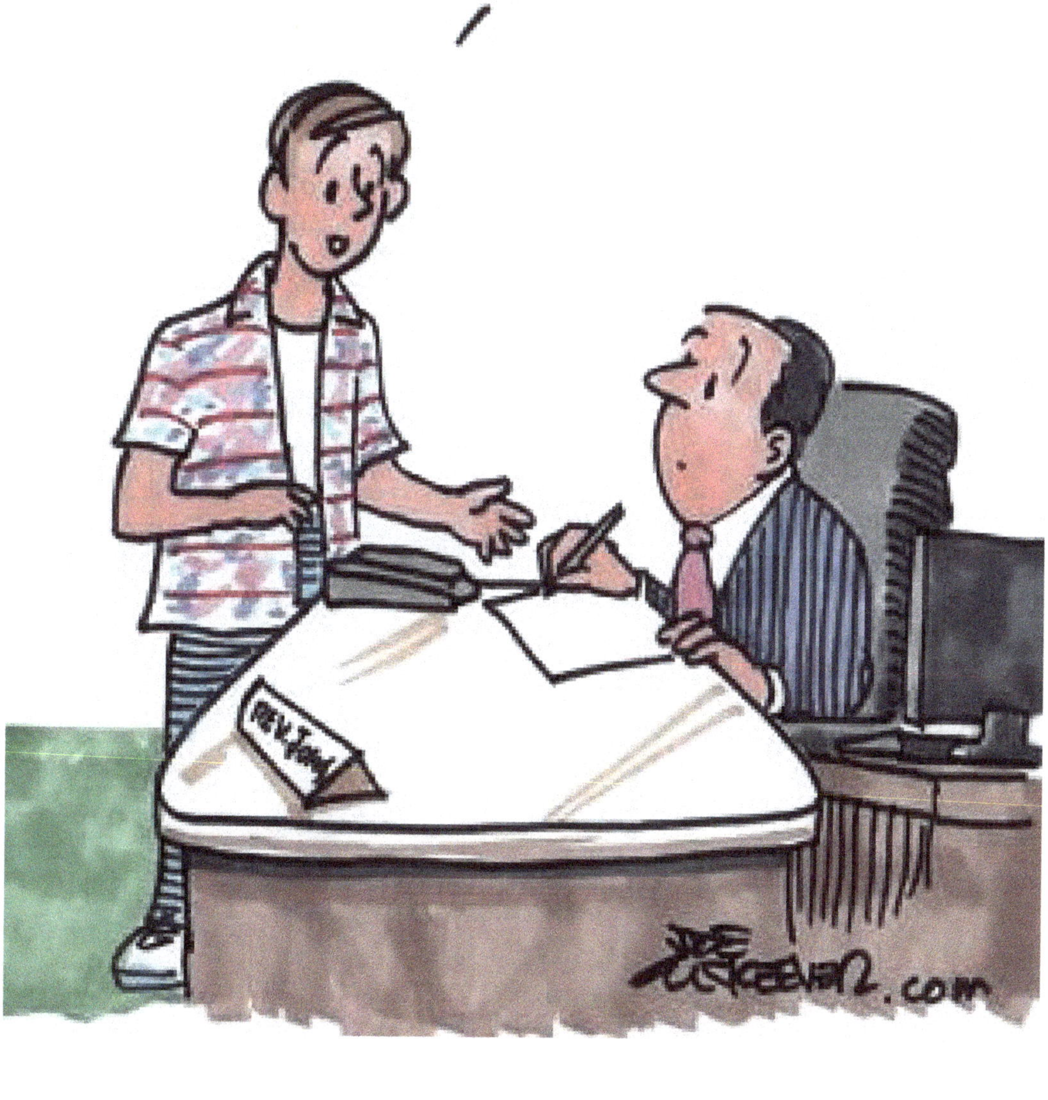

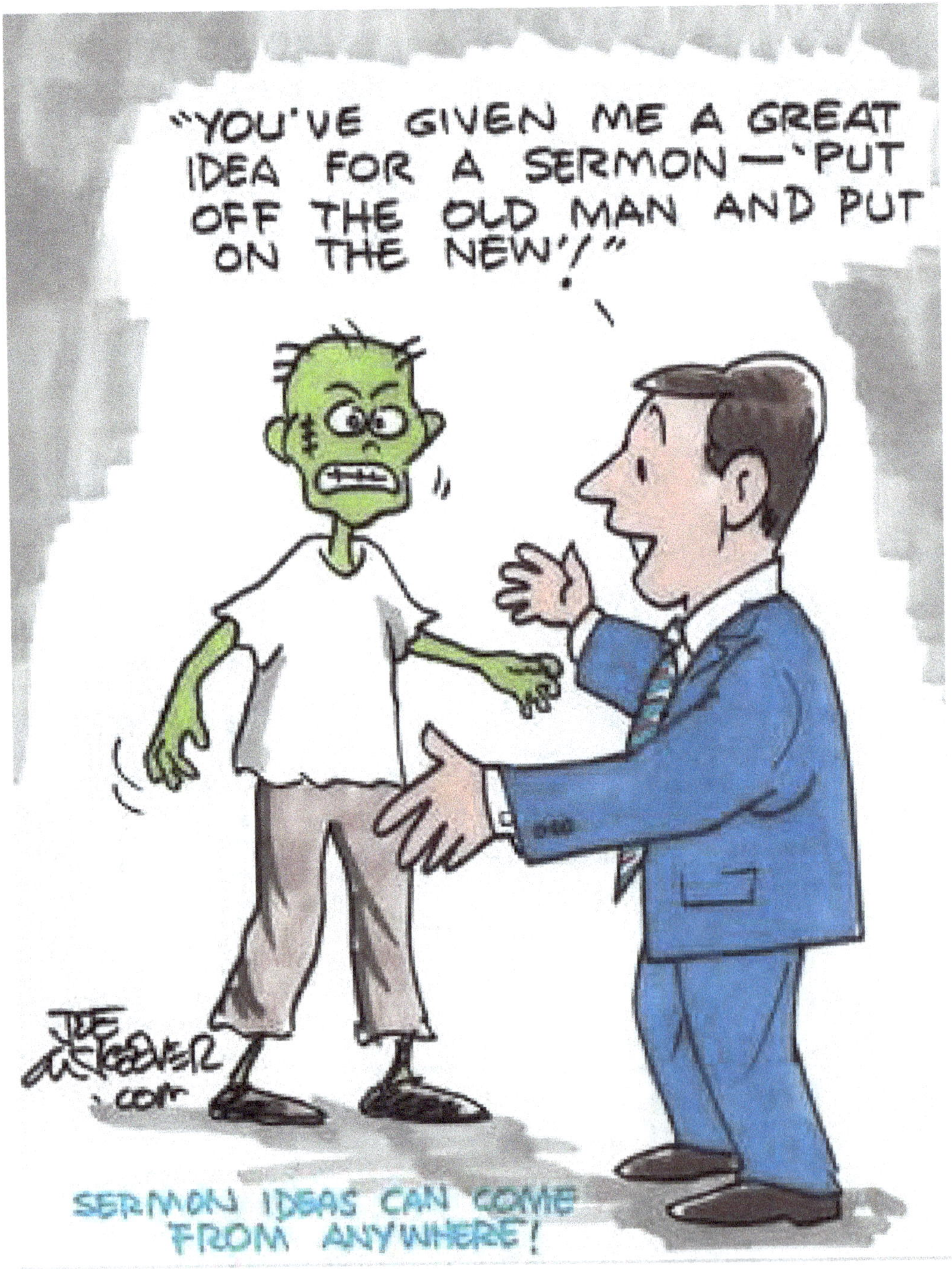
"YOU'VE GIVEN ME A GREAT IDEA FOR A SERMON—'PUT OFF THE OLD MAN AND PUT ON THE NEW'!"
JOE McKEEVER .com
SERMON IDEAS CAN COME FROM ANYWHERE!

"WELL, AFTER VISITING THE CHURCH-IN-THE-WOODS, WE WORSHIPED AT THE CHURCH-IN-THE-MALL. NOW WE'RE LOOKING FOR A CHURCH-IN-THE-WORD."

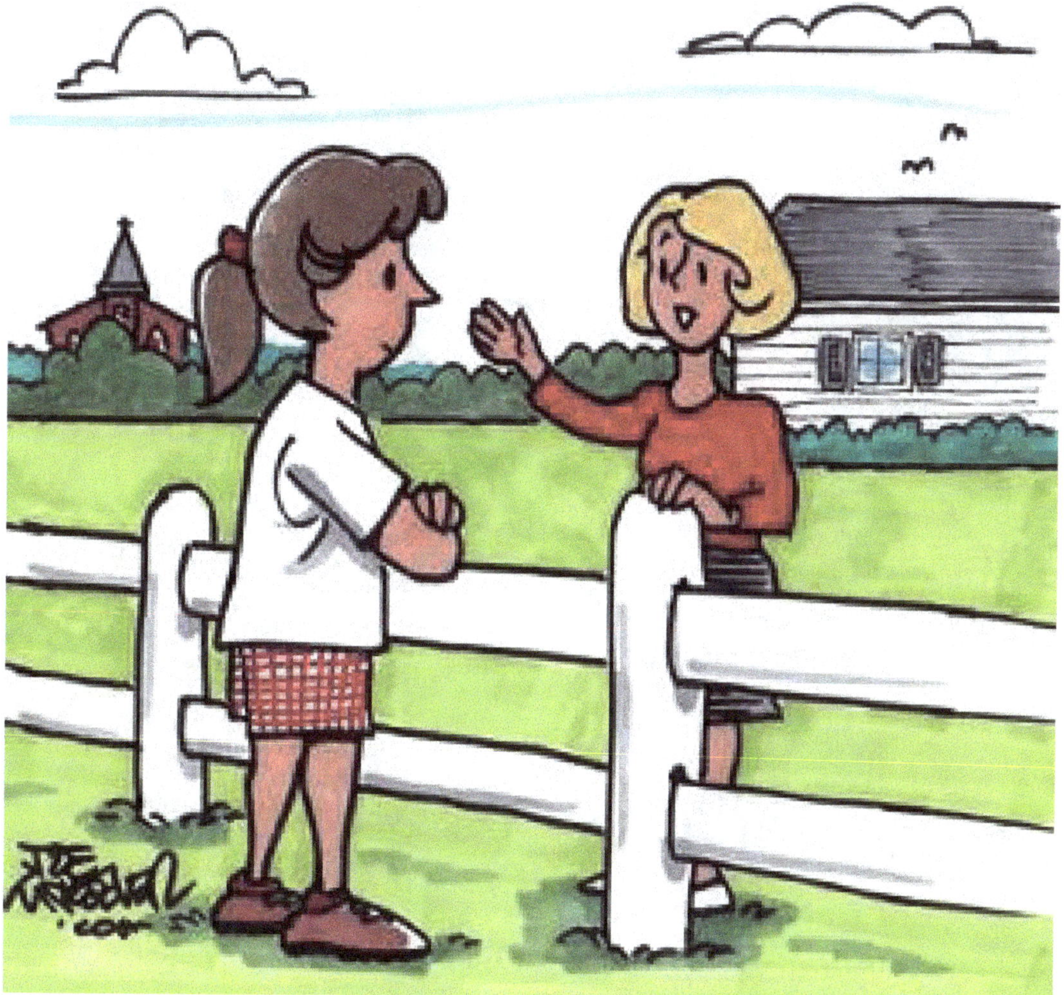

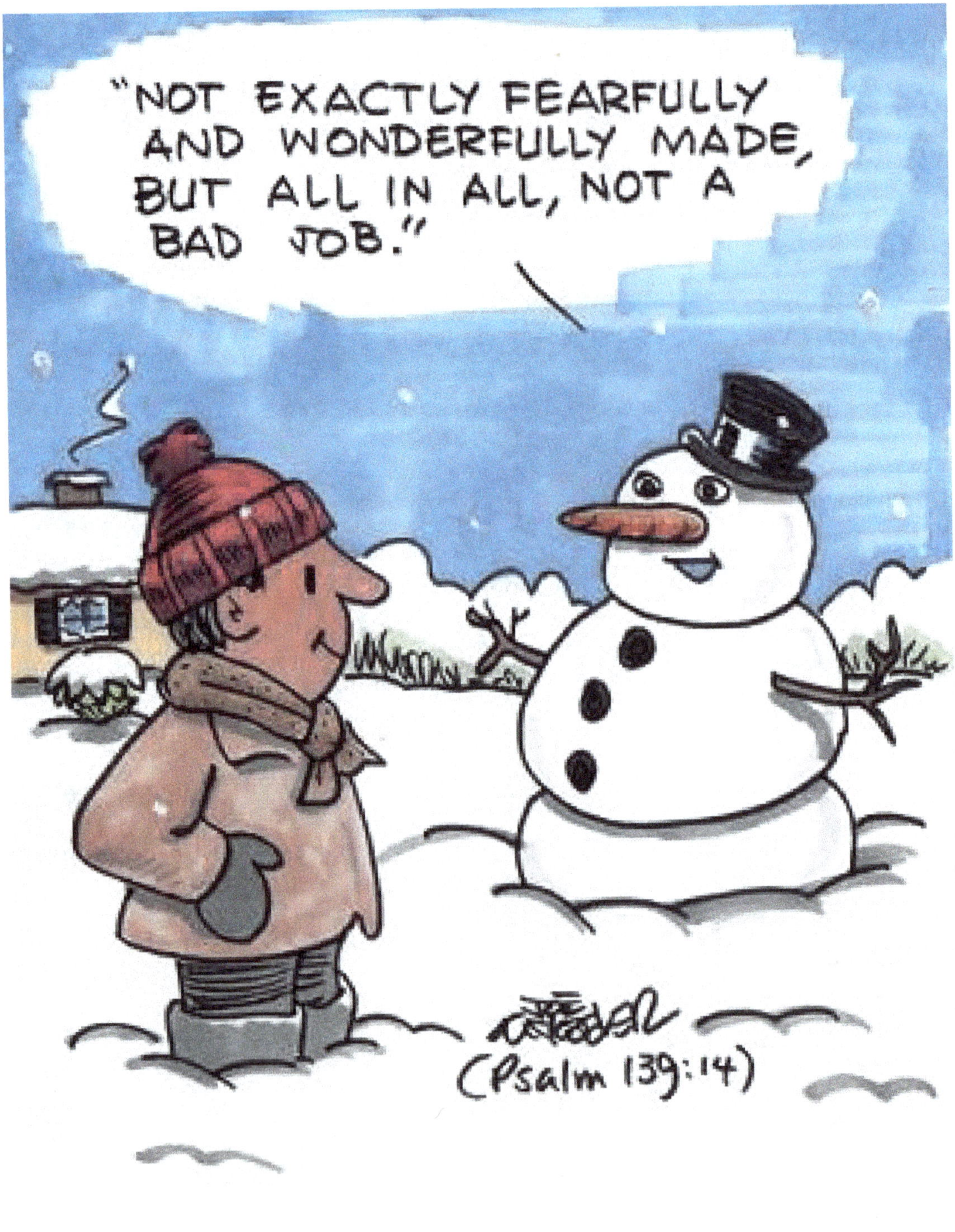
"NOT EXACTLY FEARFULLY AND WONDERFULLY MADE, BUT ALL IN ALL, NOT A BAD JOB."
(Psalm 139:14)

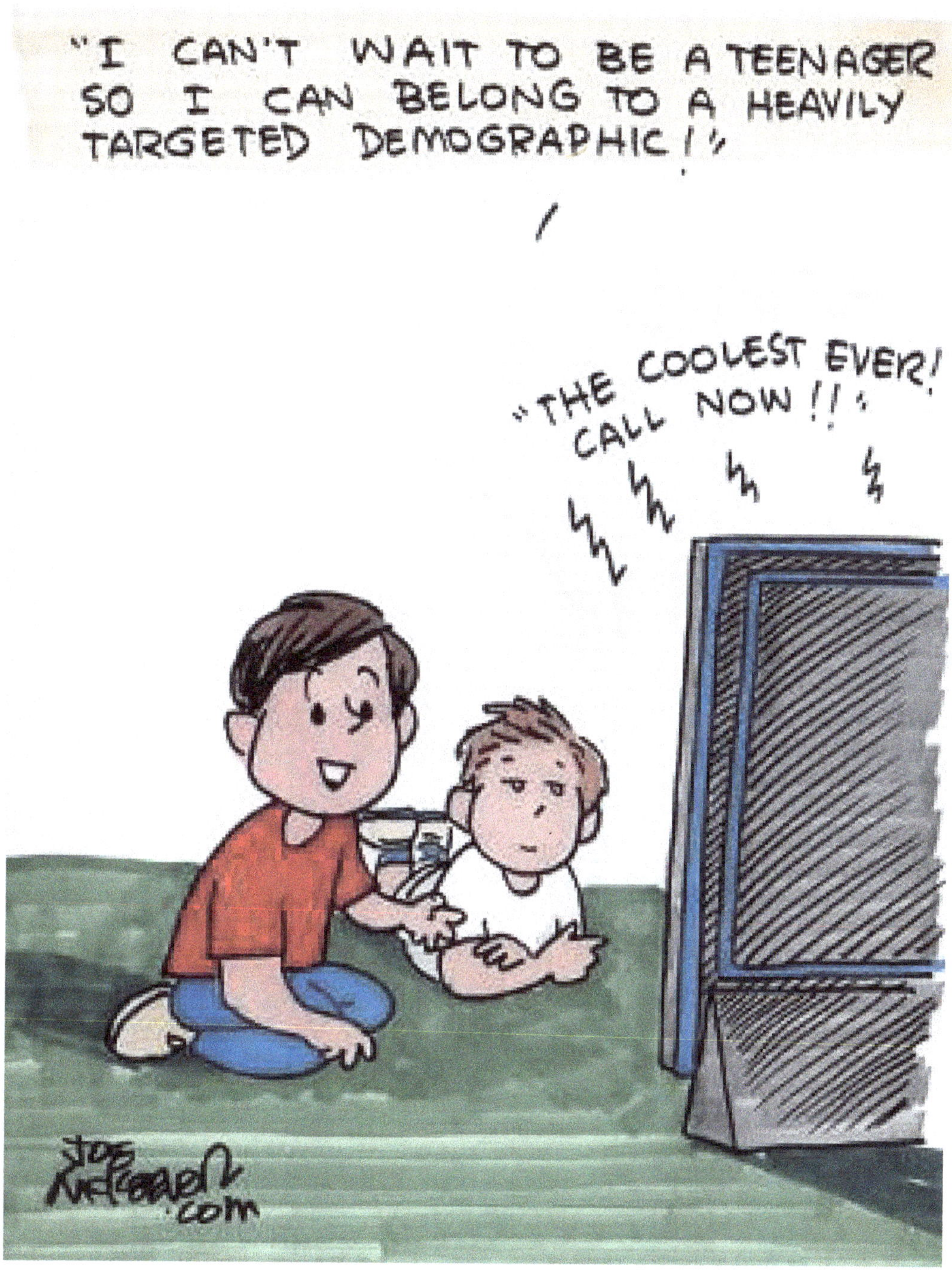
"I CAN'T WAIT TO BE A TEENAGER SO I CAN BELONG TO A HEAVILY TARGETED DEMOGRAPHIC!"
"THE COOLEST EVER! CALL NOW!!"
JOE McKEEVER.com

"I'M TELLING MY FACEBOOK FRIENDS WHAT YOU SAID. THEY ALWAYS ENJOY A GOOD LAUGH."

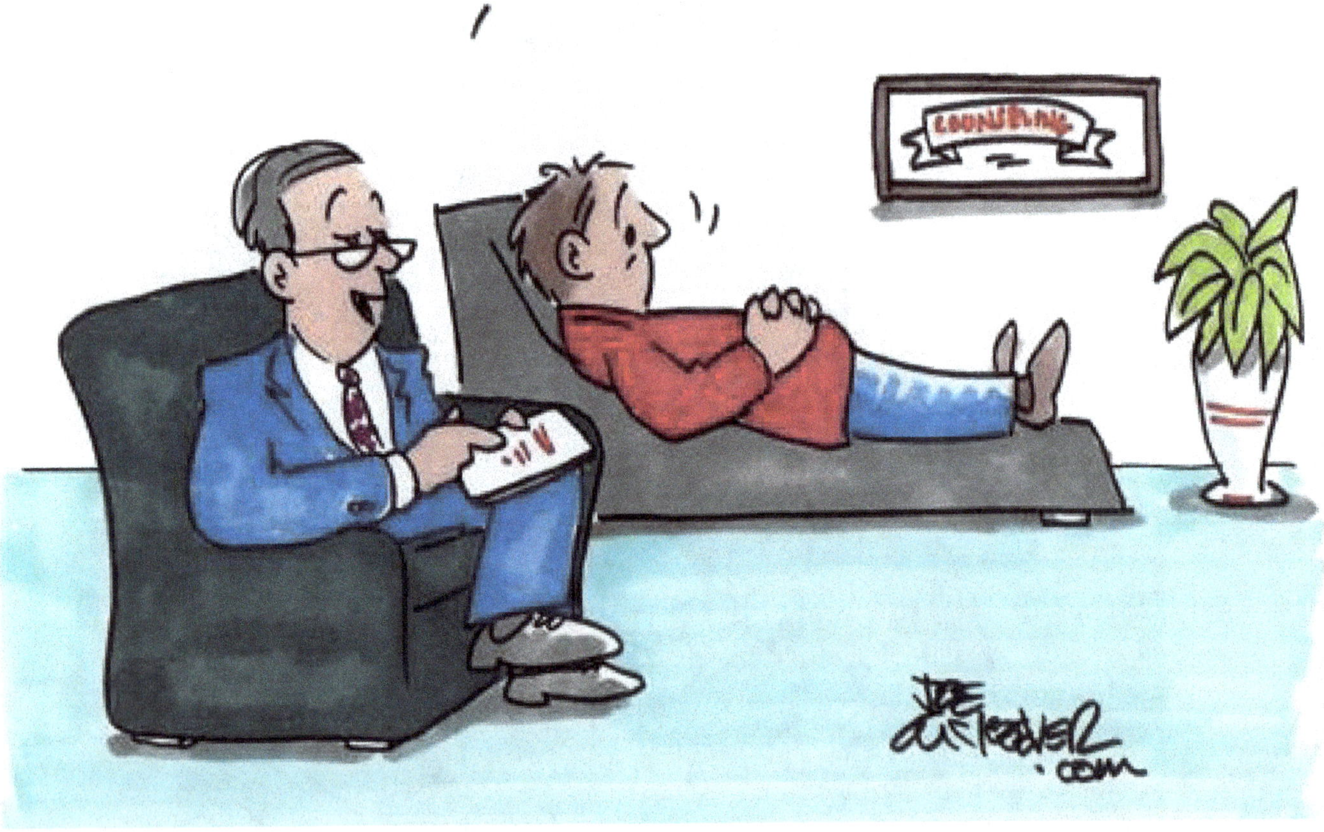

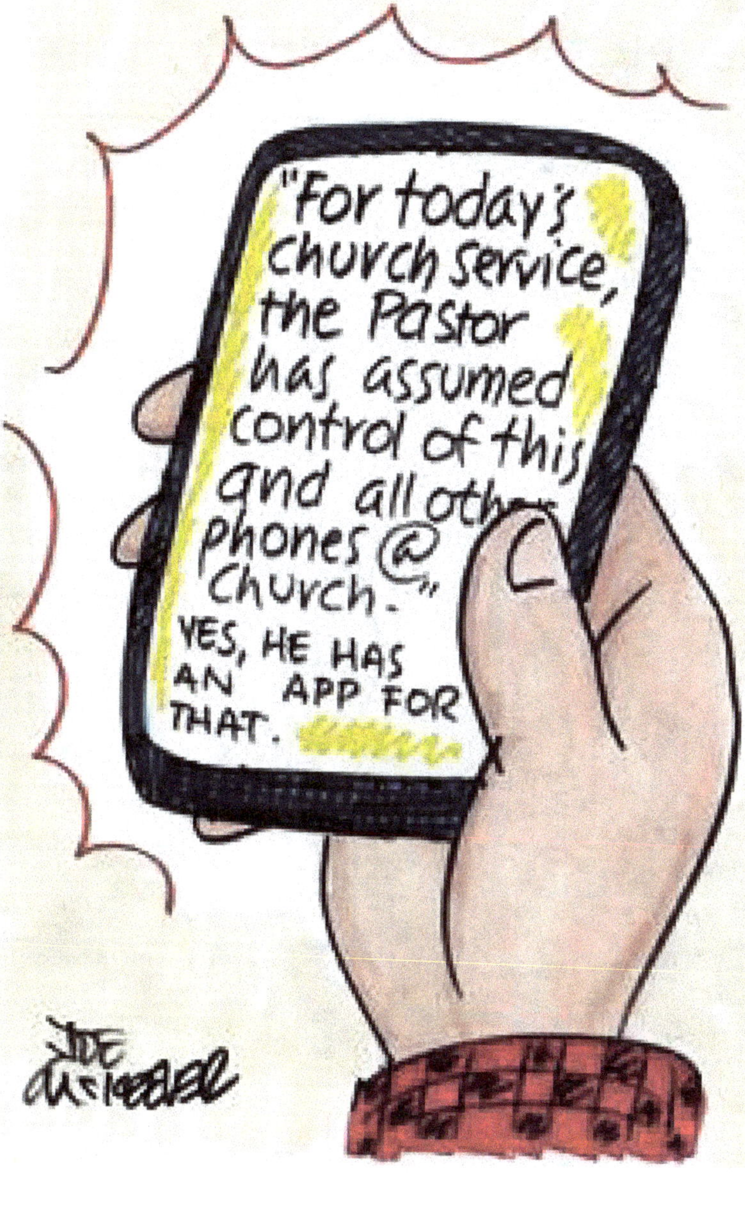
"For today's church service, the Pastor has assumed control of this and all other phones @ church."
YES, HE HAS AN APP FOR THAT.
JOE McKEEVER

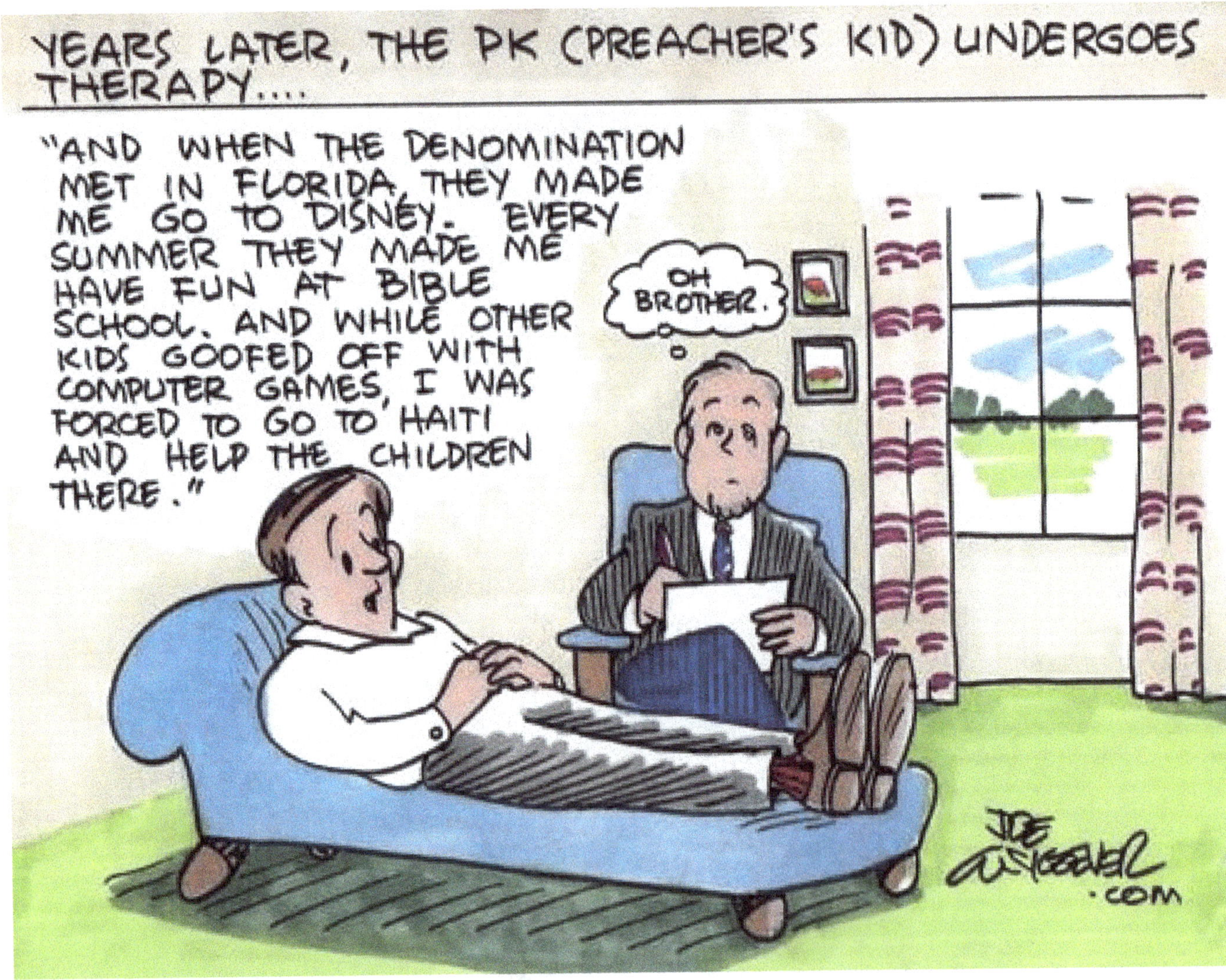
YEARS LATER, THE PK (PREACHER'S KID) UNDERGOES THERAPY....
"AND WHEN THE DENOMINATION MET IN FLORIDA, THEY MADE ME GO TO DISNEY. EVERY SUMMER THEY MADE ME HAVE FUN AT BIBLE SCHOOL. AND WHILE OTHER KIDS GOOFED OFF WITH COMPUTER GAMES, I WAS FORCED TO GO TO HAITI AND HELP THE CHILDREN THERE."
OH BROTHER.
.COM

"WHAT MAKES THIS WORSE IS THAT THERE IS NO CELEBRITY FOUNDATION FINANCING RESEARCH ON YOUR CONDITION."

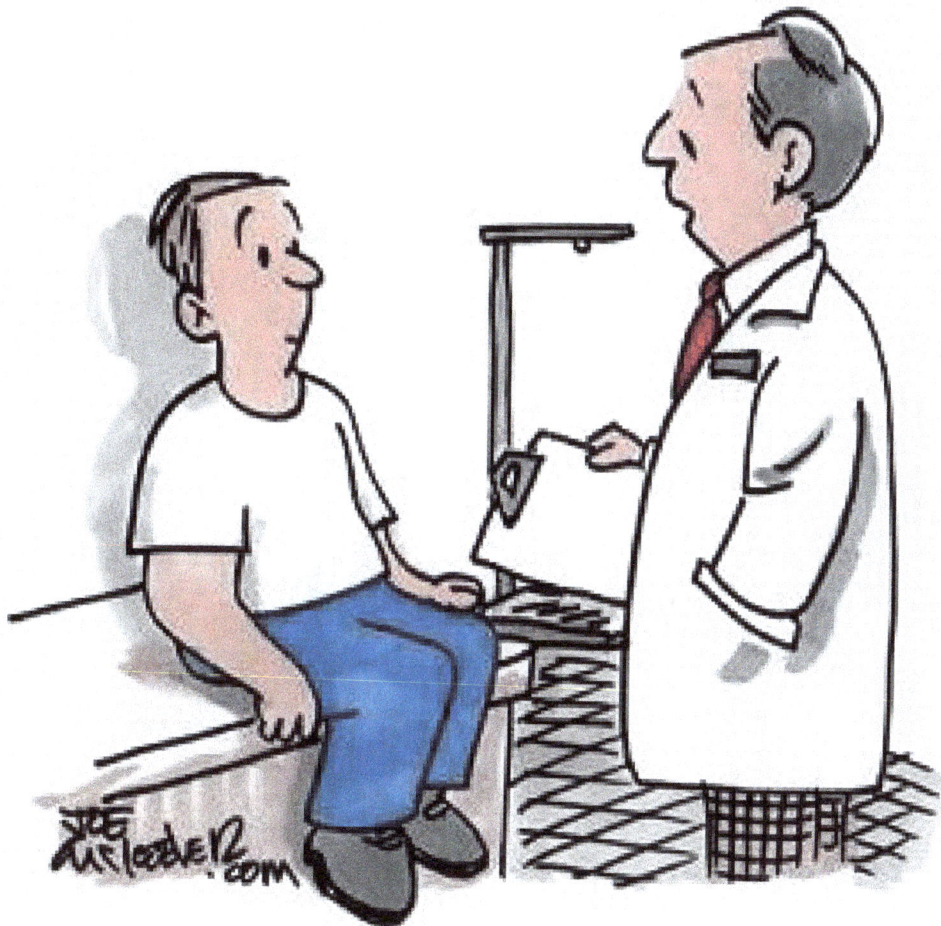

"PASTOR, YOU REMEMBER ROGER AIREDALE, THE BIG-SHOT WHO GOT YOU FIRED FROM YOUR LAST TWO CHURCHES."

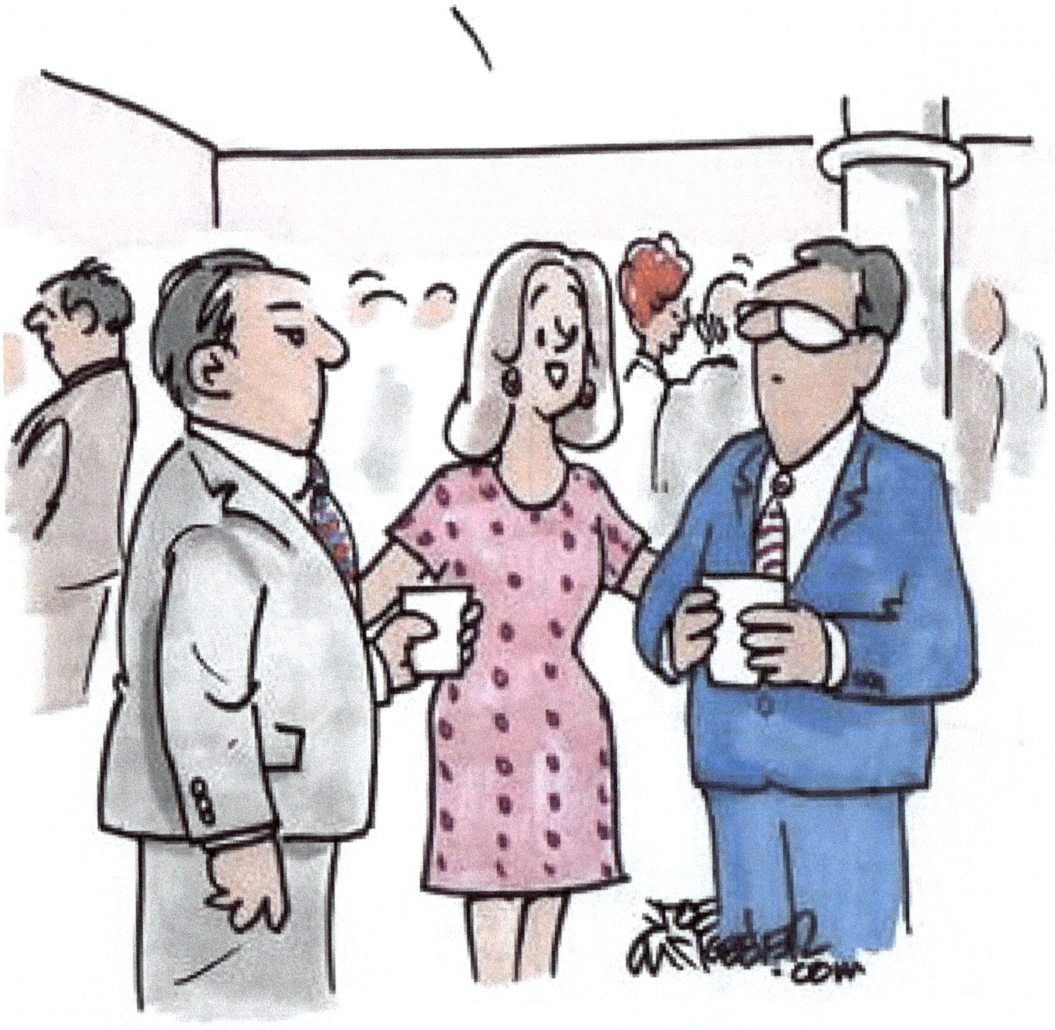

"MAYBE," PASTOR TIM THOUGHT, "COMING TO THE BEACH TO WORK ON HIS SERMON ON SUFFERING AND PERSECUTION WAS NOT A GOOD IDEA AFTER ALL."

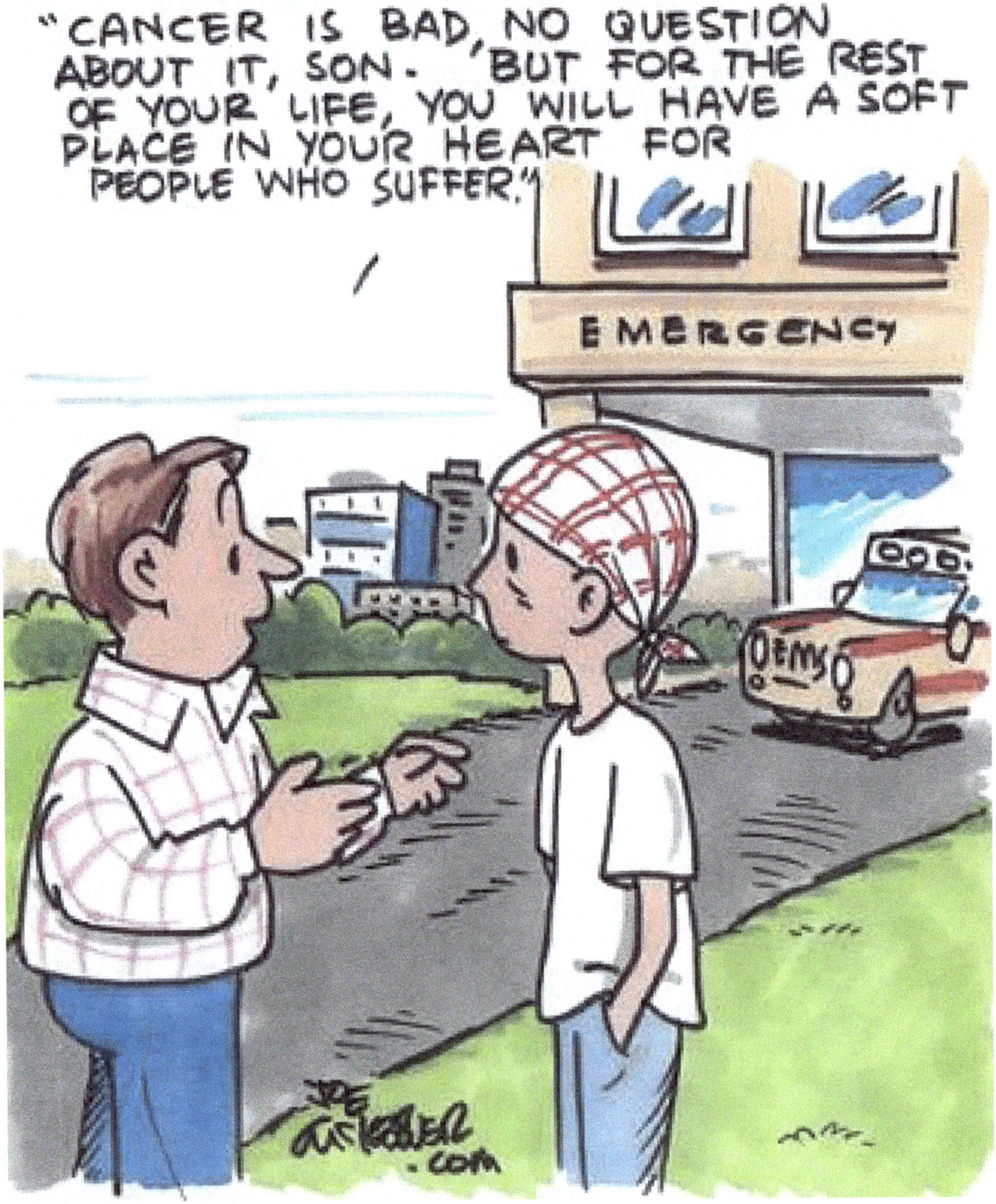
"CANCER IS BAD, NO QUESTION ABOUT IT, SON. BUT FOR THE REST OF YOUR LIFE, YOU WILL HAVE A SOFT PLACE IN YOUR HEART FOR PEOPLE WHO SUFFER."
EMERGENCY
EMS

-COMICS-
BABY BLUES
"I BELIEVE IN GOD. DON'T YOU?"
"SURE. I DO."
HI AND LOIS
I WANT TO GO TO CHURCH, HI!
WHY?
We're Drawn that way!!
Apologies! JOE

"GOOD MORNING, FIRST NATIONAL CHURCH, PREVIOUSLY KNOWN AS THE CHURCH IN THE MALL, AND BEFORE THAT, SHILOH MISSIONARY CHURCH NUMBER TWO! TO WHOM SHALL I DIRECT YOUR CALL?"

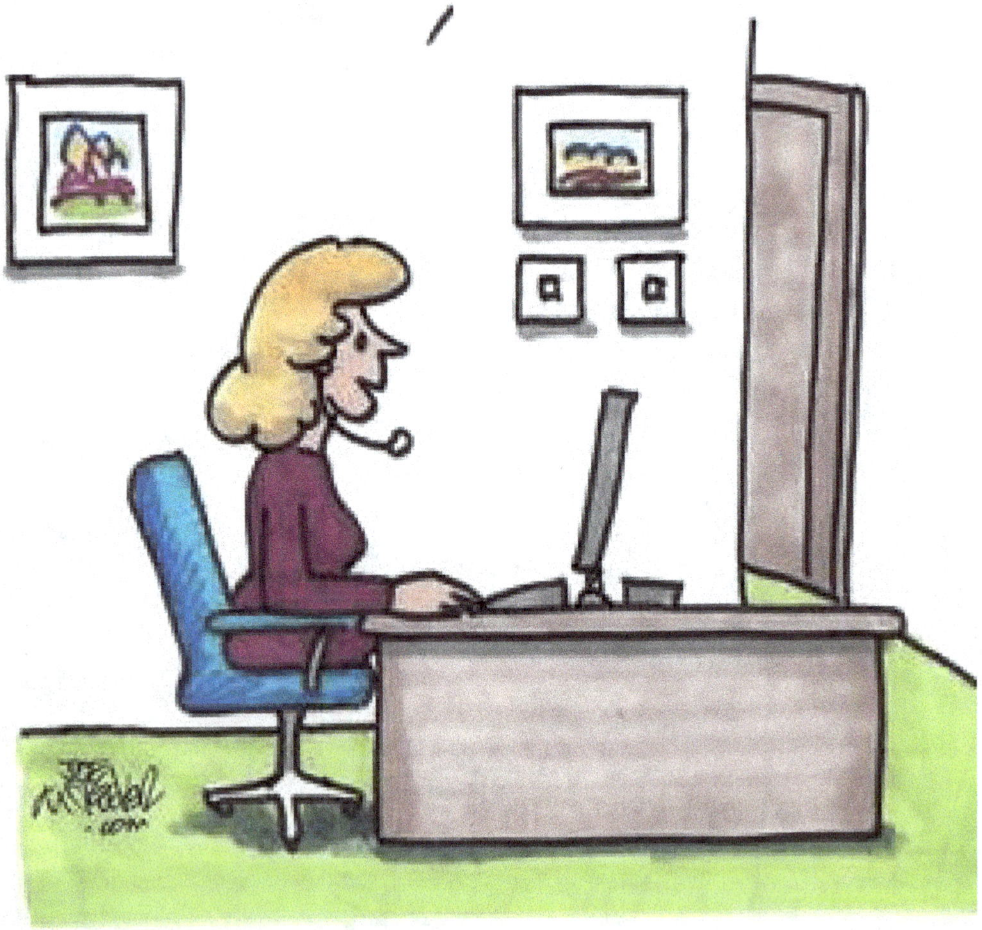

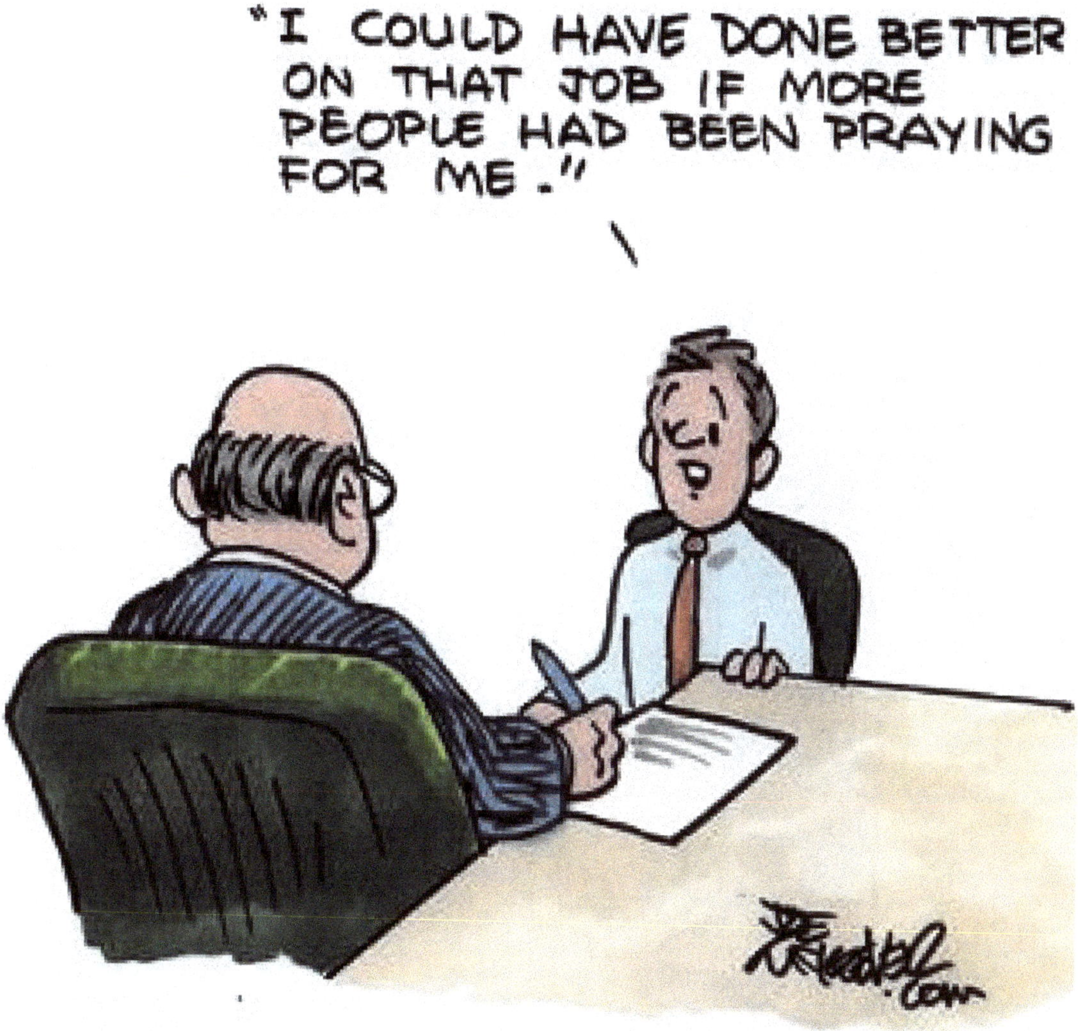
"I COULD HAVE DONE BETTER ON THAT JOB IF MORE PEOPLE HAD BEEN PRAYING FOR ME."

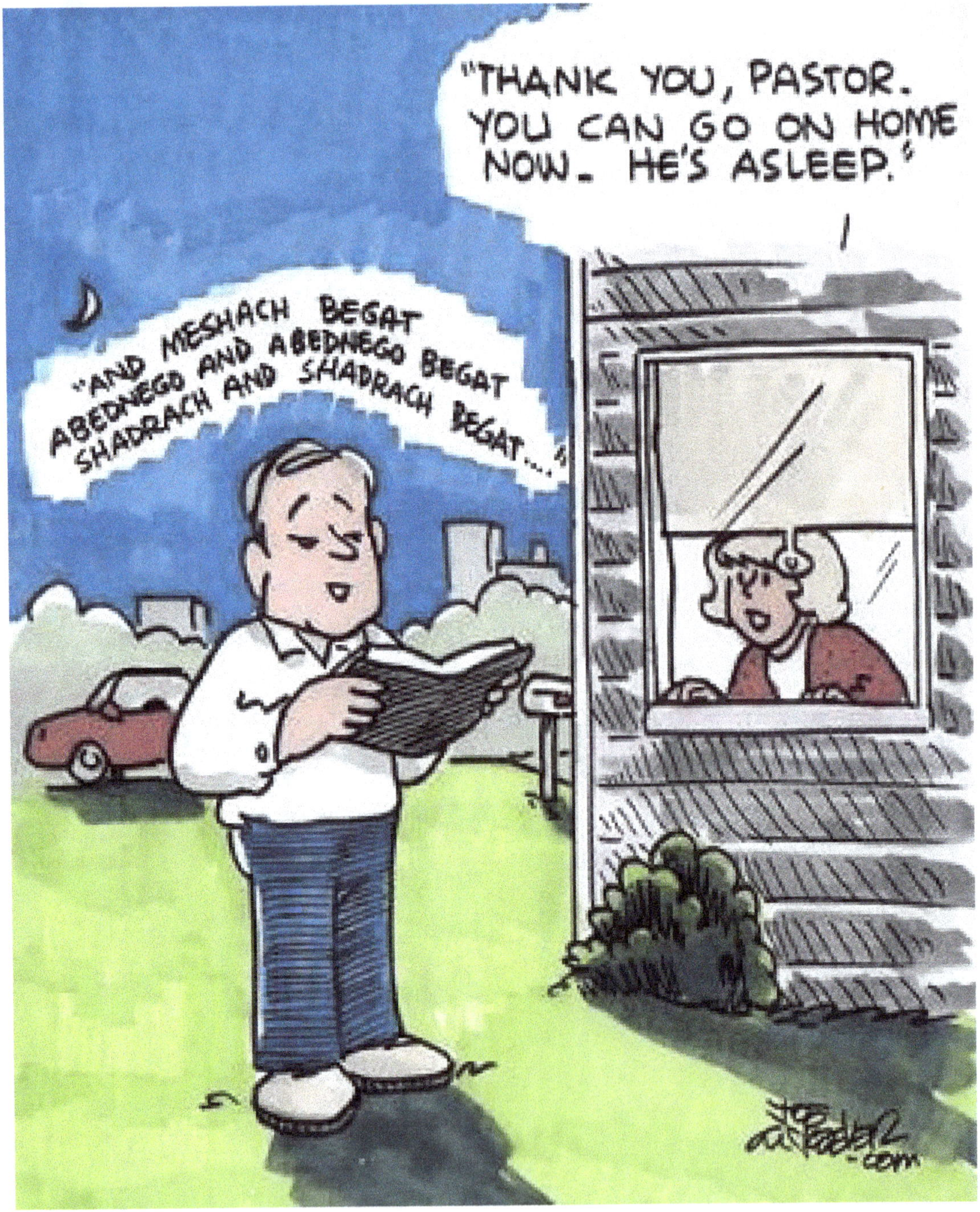
"THANK YOU, PASTOR. YOU CAN GO ON HOME NOW. HE'S ASLEEP."
"AND MESHACH BEGAT ABEDNEGO AND ABEDNEGO BEGAT SHADRACH AND SHADRACH BEGAT..."

"IT'S GOING TO TAKE A GREAT SERMON, PASTOR, FOR YOU TO OUTPREACH THAT TIE!"

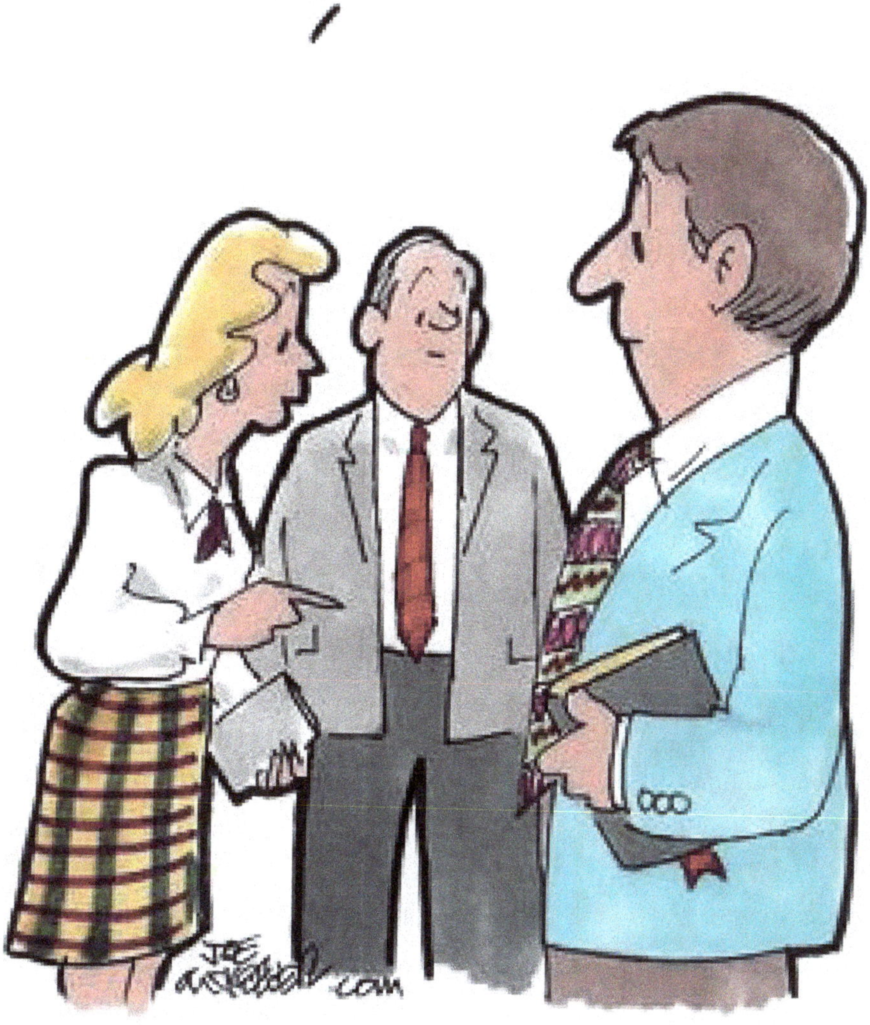

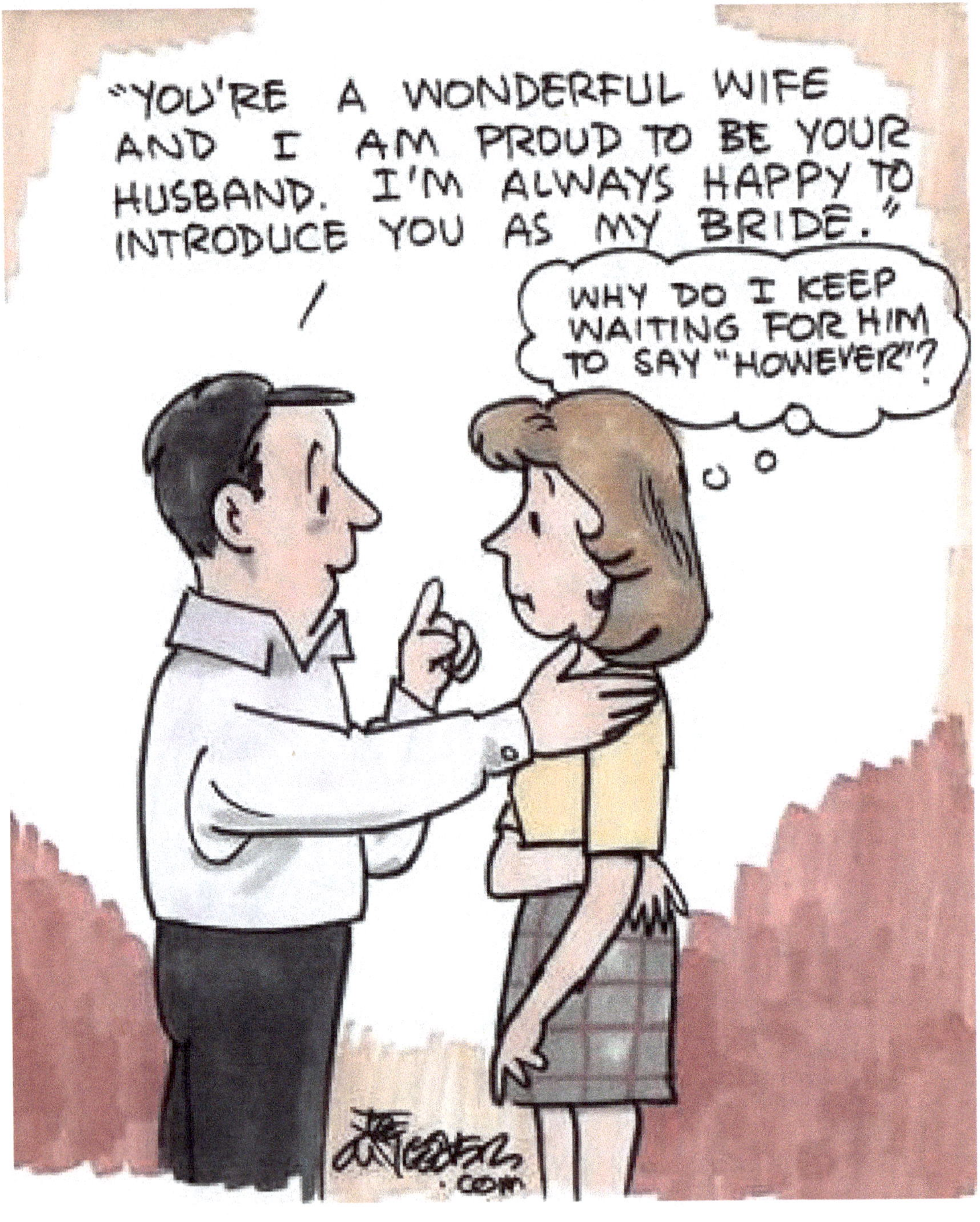
"YOU'RE A WONDERFUL WIFE AND I AM PROUD TO BE YOUR HUSBAND. I'M ALWAYS HAPPY TO INTRODUCE YOU AS MY BRIDE."
WHY DO I KEEP WAITING FOR HIM TO SAY "HOWEVER"?
.com

"WE BOUGHT THEM FROM A TAVERN THAT WENT BELLY-UP WHEN WE CONVERTED ALL THEIR CUSTOMERS. OUR PEOPLE FEEL RIGHT AT HOME."

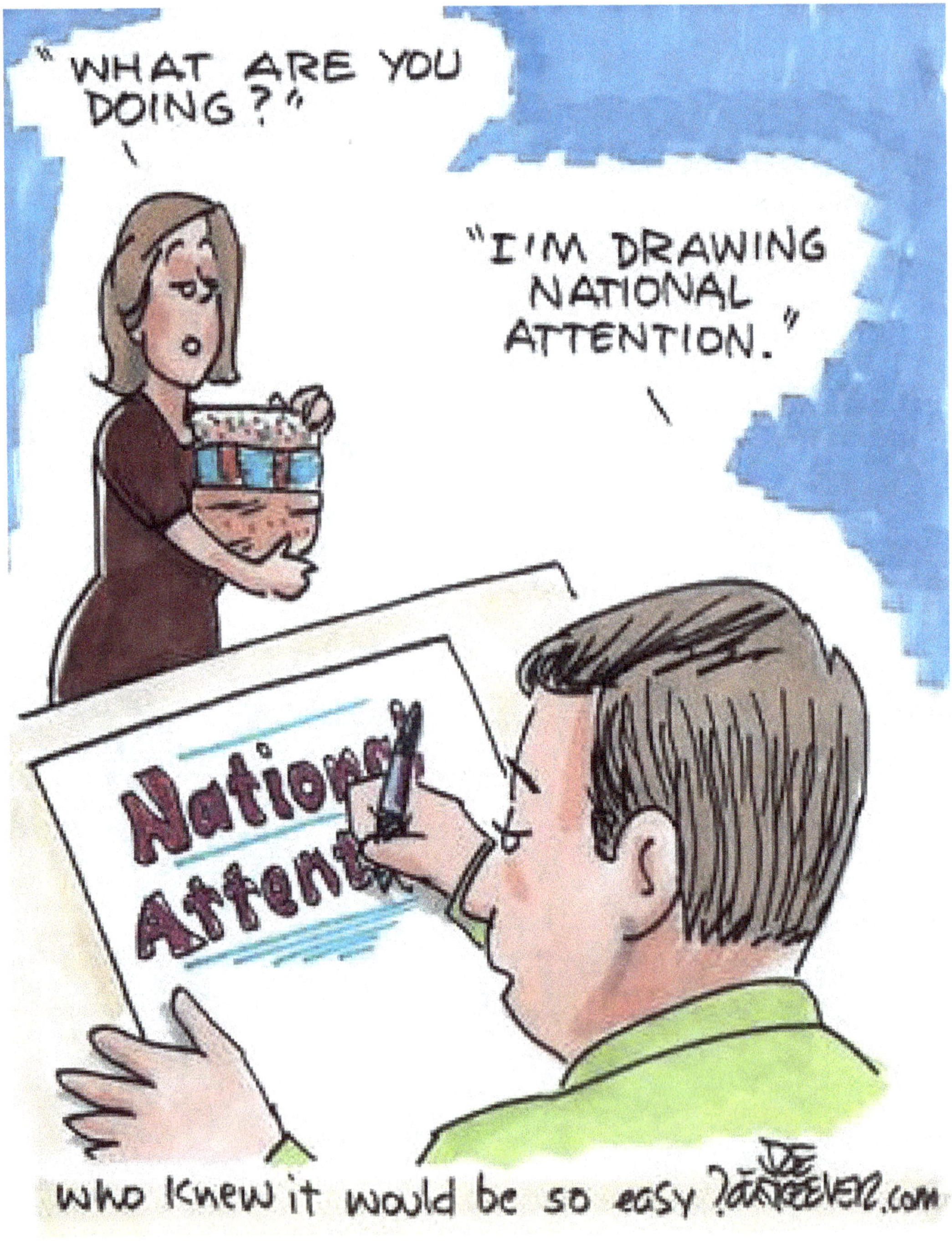
"WHAT ARE YOU DOING?"
"I'M DRAWING NATIONAL ATTENTION."
National Attent
who knew it would be so easy?

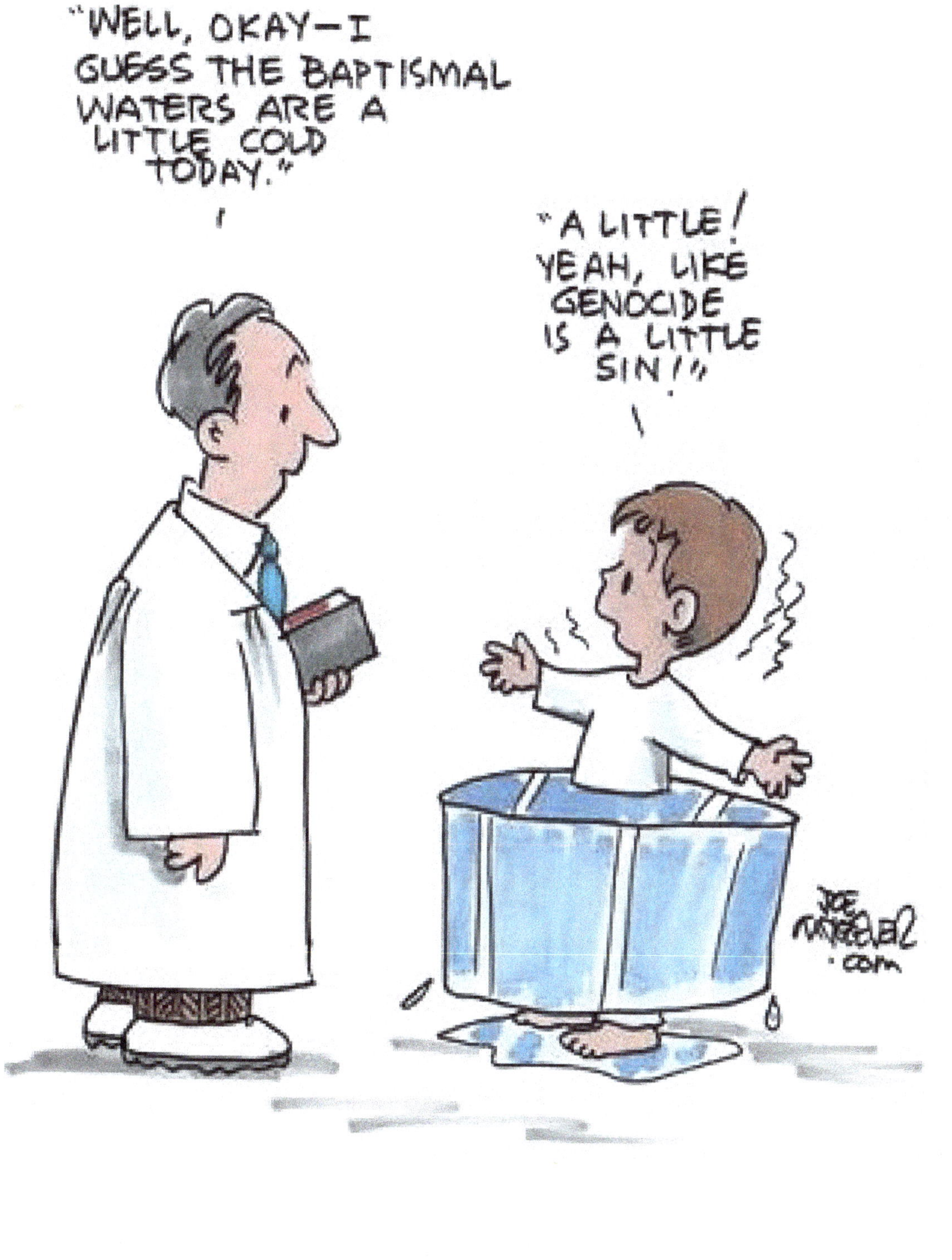
"WELL, OKAY—I GUESS THE BAPTISMAL WATERS ARE A LITTLE COLD TODAY."
"A LITTLE! YEAH, LIKE GENOCIDE IS A LITTLE SIN!"
JOE MCKEEVER .com

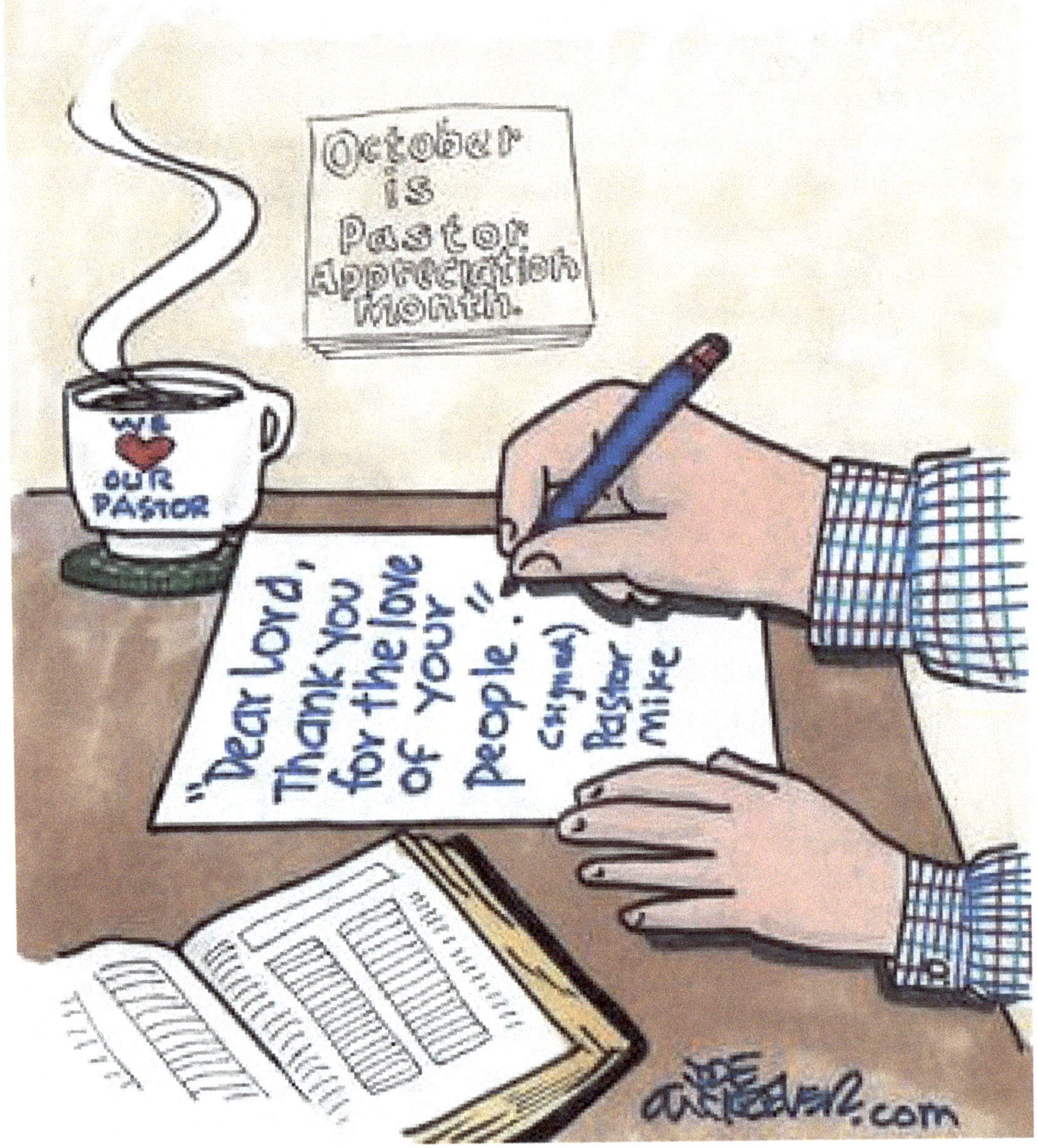
October is Pastor Appreciation month.
WE ♥ OUR PASTOR
"Dear Lord, Thank you for the love of your people."
(signed) Pastor Mike

PASTOR APPRECIATION CAN HAPPEN ANY TIME.

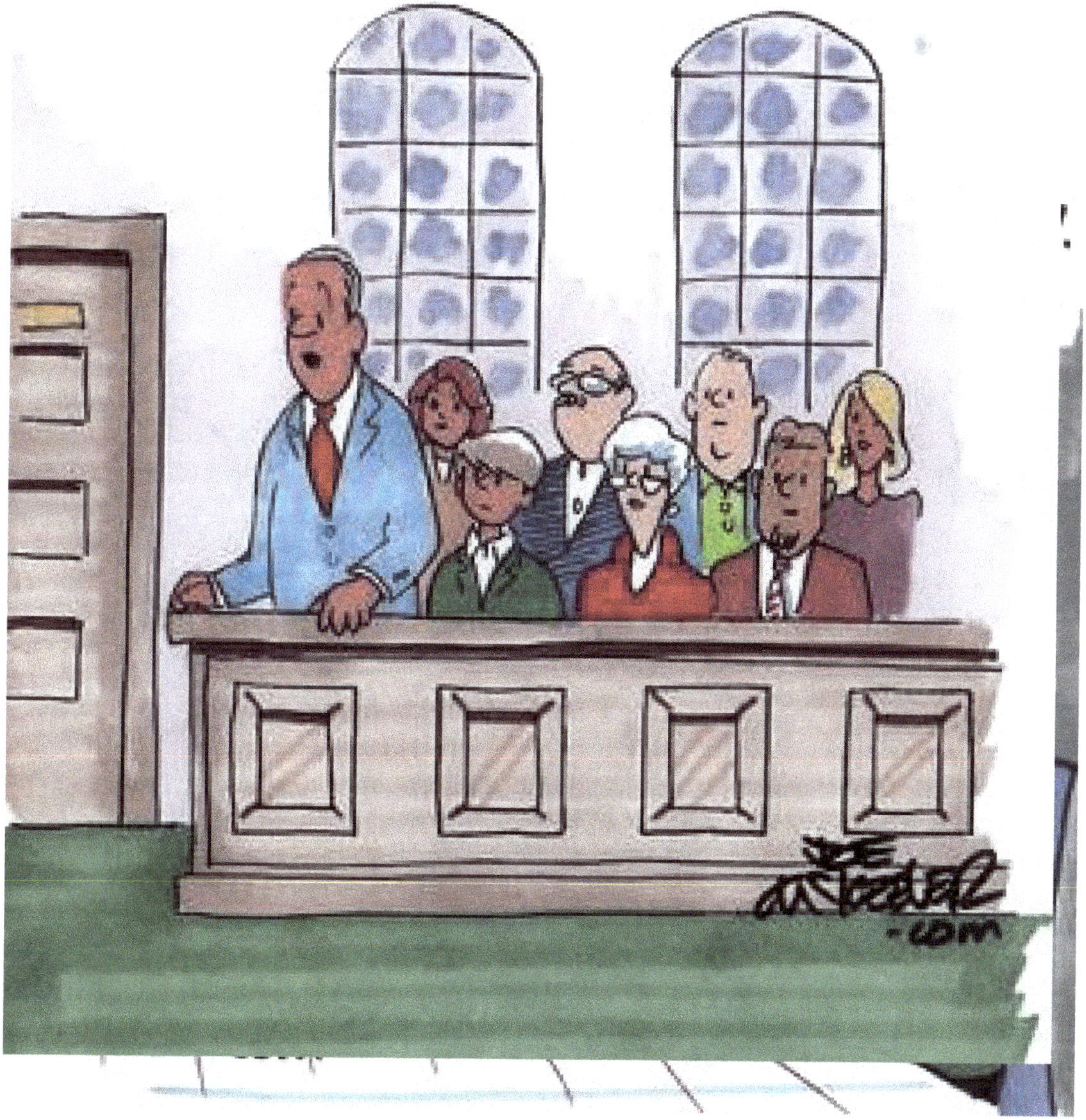

"YOUR HONOR, WE FIND THE DEFENDANT TO BE A LOT LIKE OURSELVES."

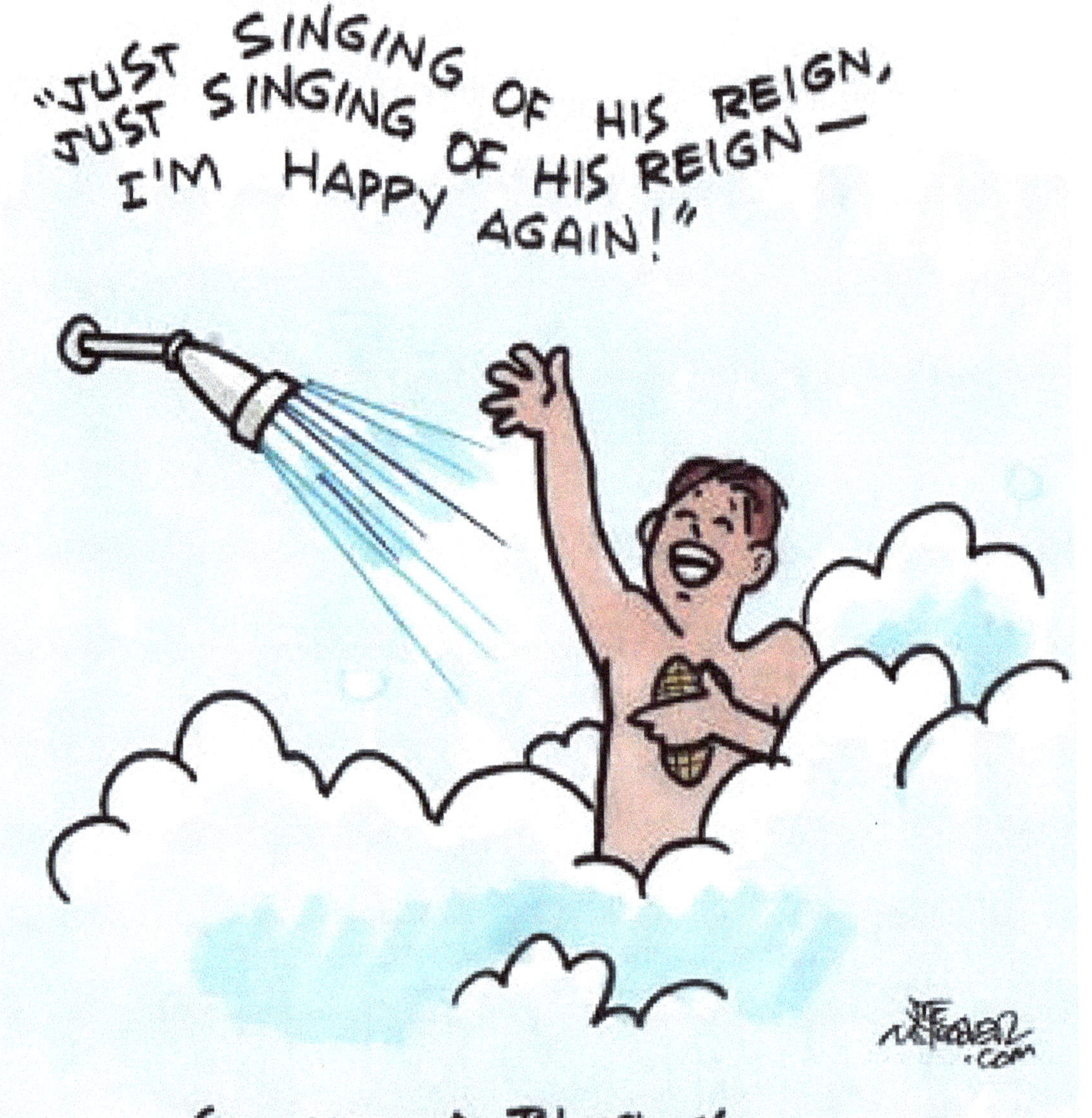
"JUST SINGING OF HIS REIGN,
JUST SINGING OF HIS REIGN—
I'M HAPPY AGAIN!"

Showers of Blessings

"I'LL TELL YOU WHY I'M NOT IN CHURCH, PASTOR — THE SEEKER CHURCH DOESN'T DISCIPLE PEOPLE, THE TEACHING CHURCH ISN'T EVANGELISTIC, THE MEGACHURCH IS ALL ABOUT SHOW, SMALL CHURCHES ARE OUT OF TOUCH, AND THE HOUSE CHURCH IS A JOKE!"

He who needs an excuse will always find one.

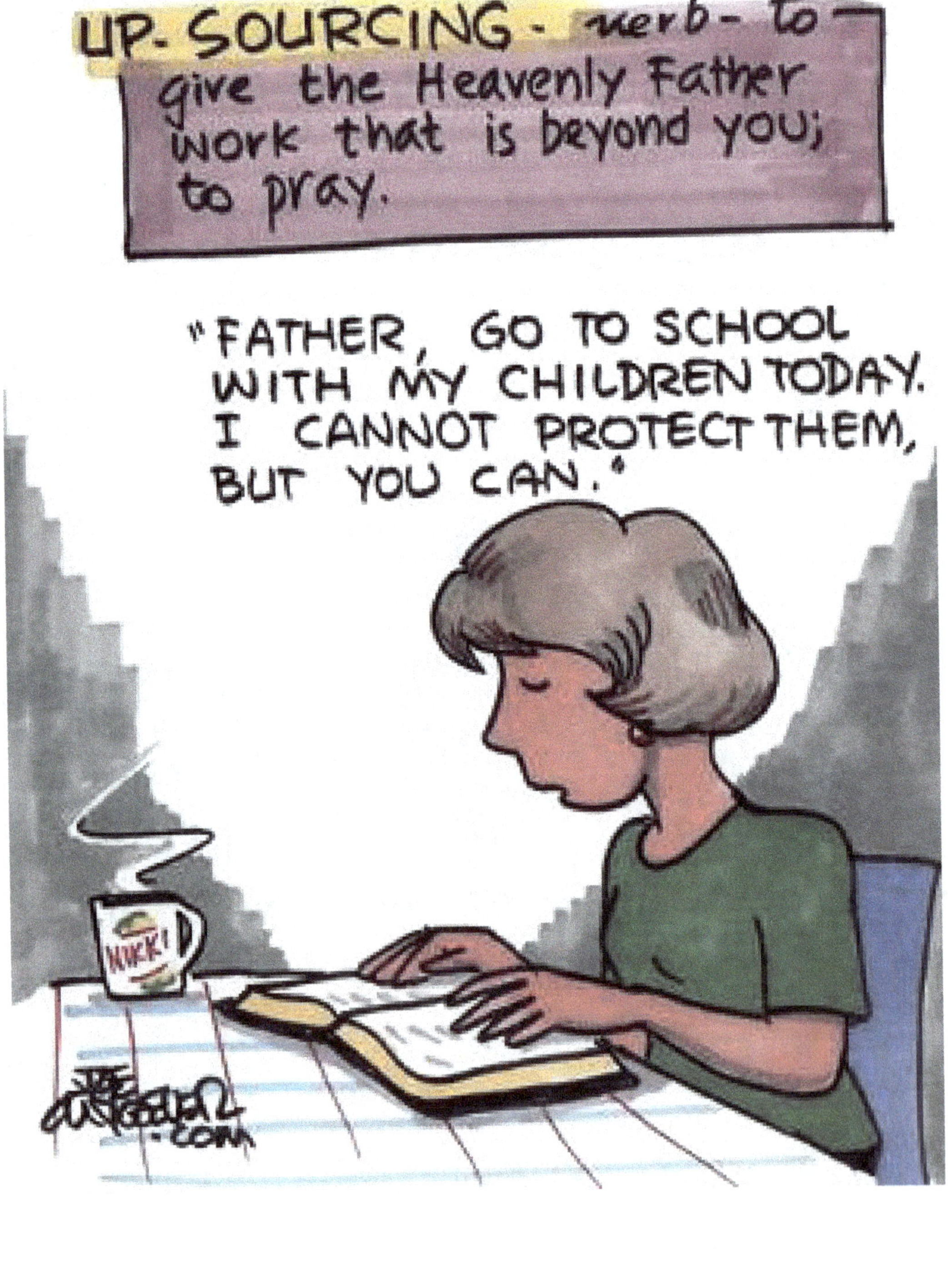
UP-SOURCING - verb - to give the Heavenly Father work that is beyond you; to pray.
"FATHER, GO TO SCHOOL WITH MY CHILDREN TODAY. I CANNOT PROTECT THEM, BUT YOU CAN."

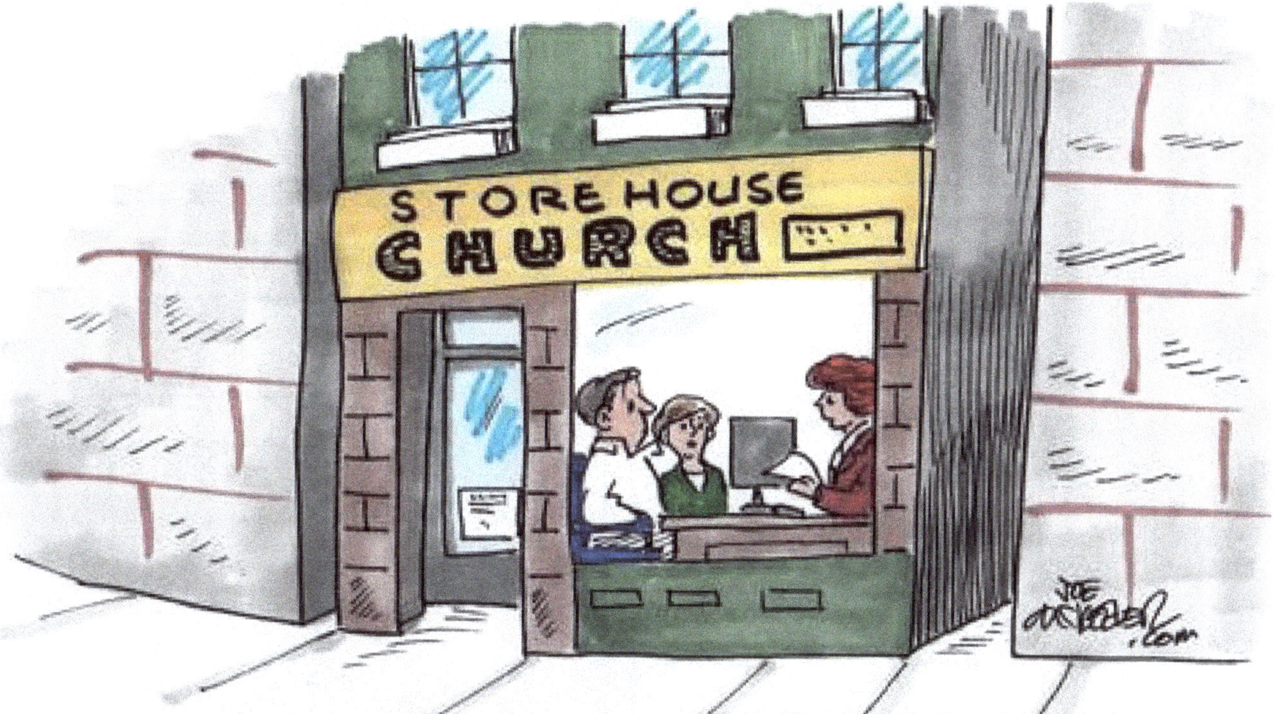
STOREHOUSE
CHURCH

"WE BEGAN AS A STOREFRONT CHURCH. THEN, READING MALACHI 3:10, WE REALIZED IF WE WERE A STOREHOUSE, PEOPLE WOULD BRING ALL THEIR TITHES HERE."

"COULD YOU COME BACK LATER? THE DOCTOR IS LATE FOR HIS TEE TIME AND I'M READY FOR MY TEA TIME."

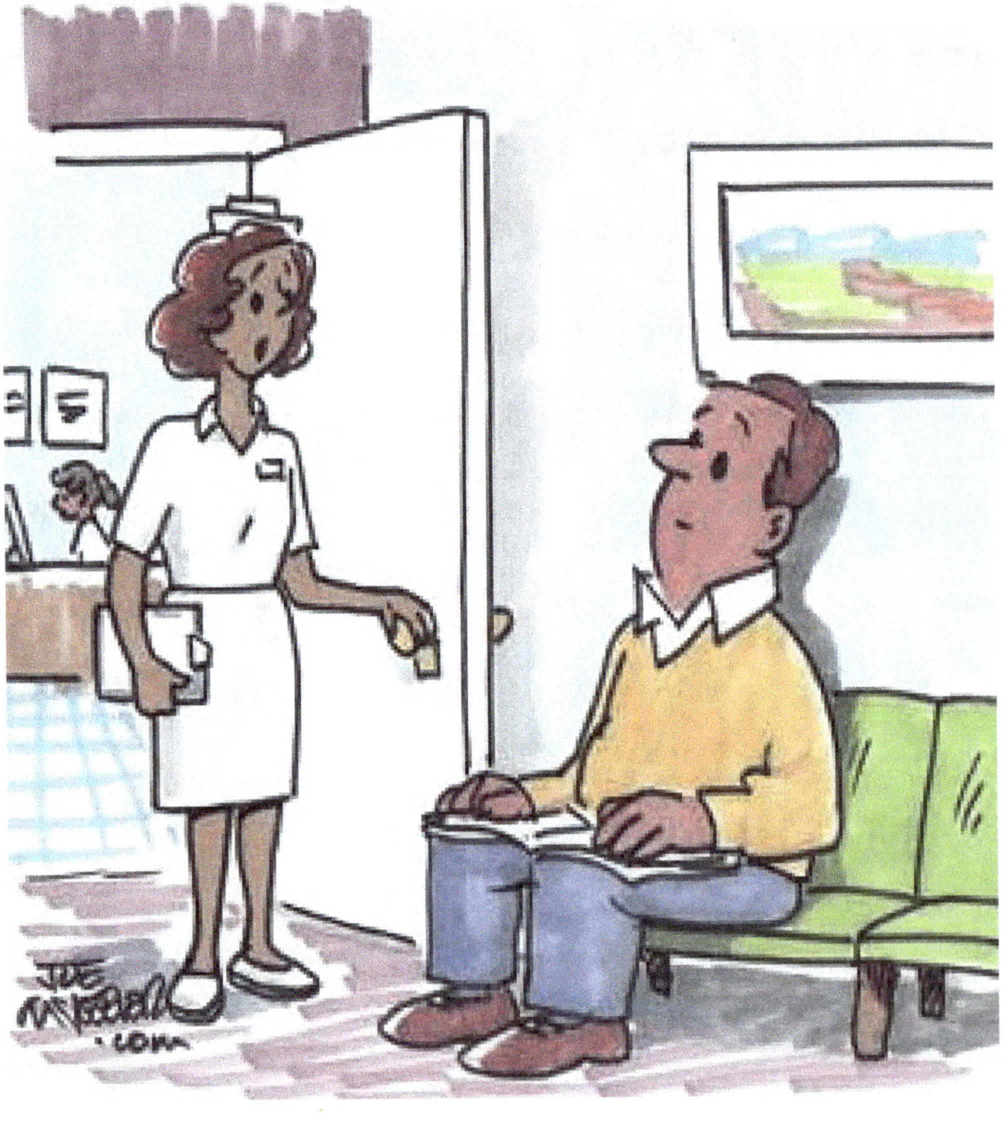

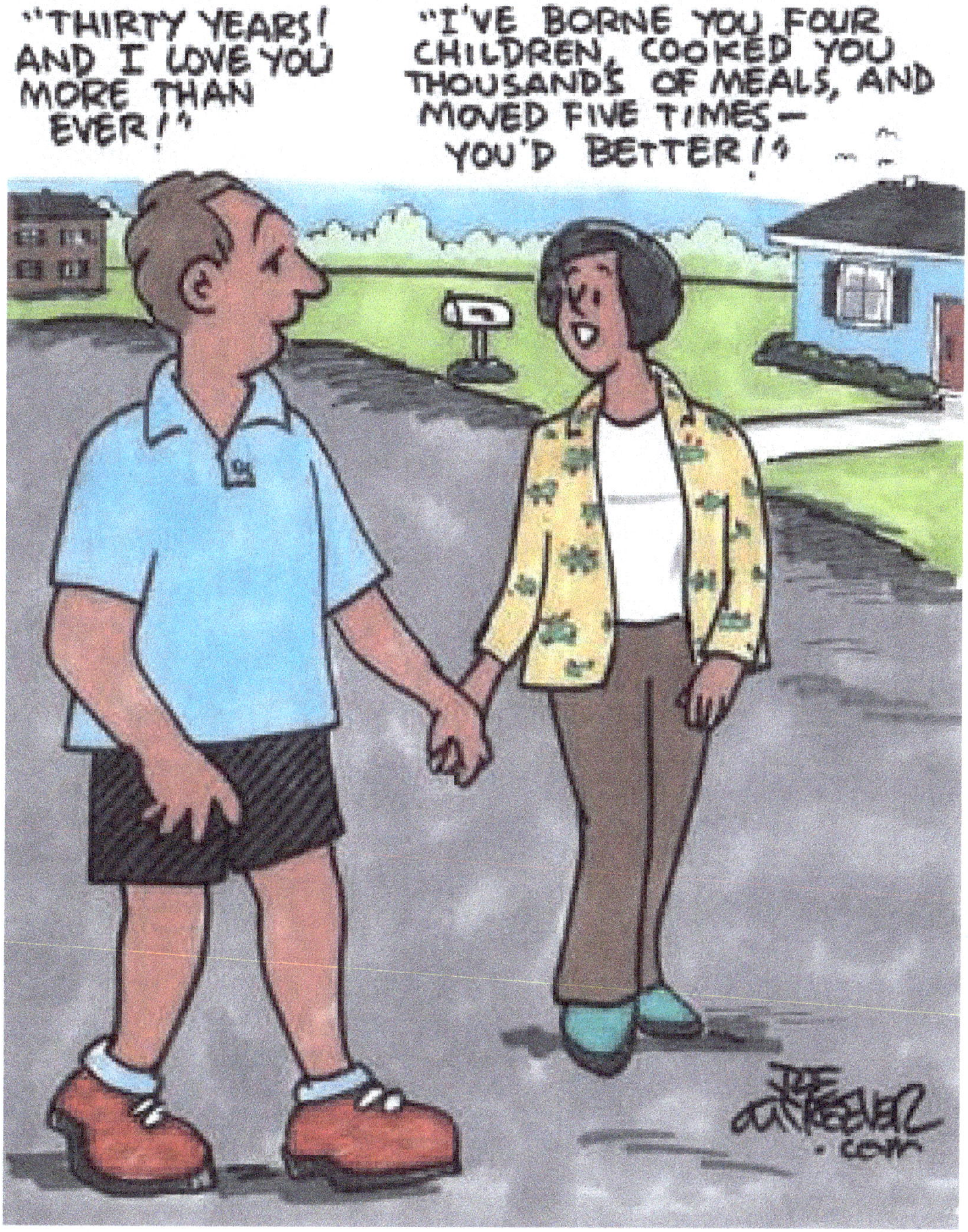
"THIRTY YEARS! AND I LOVE YOU MORE THAN EVER!"
"I'VE BORNE YOU FOUR CHILDREN, COOKED YOU THOUSANDS OF MEALS, AND MOVED FIVE TIMES— YOU'D BETTER!"

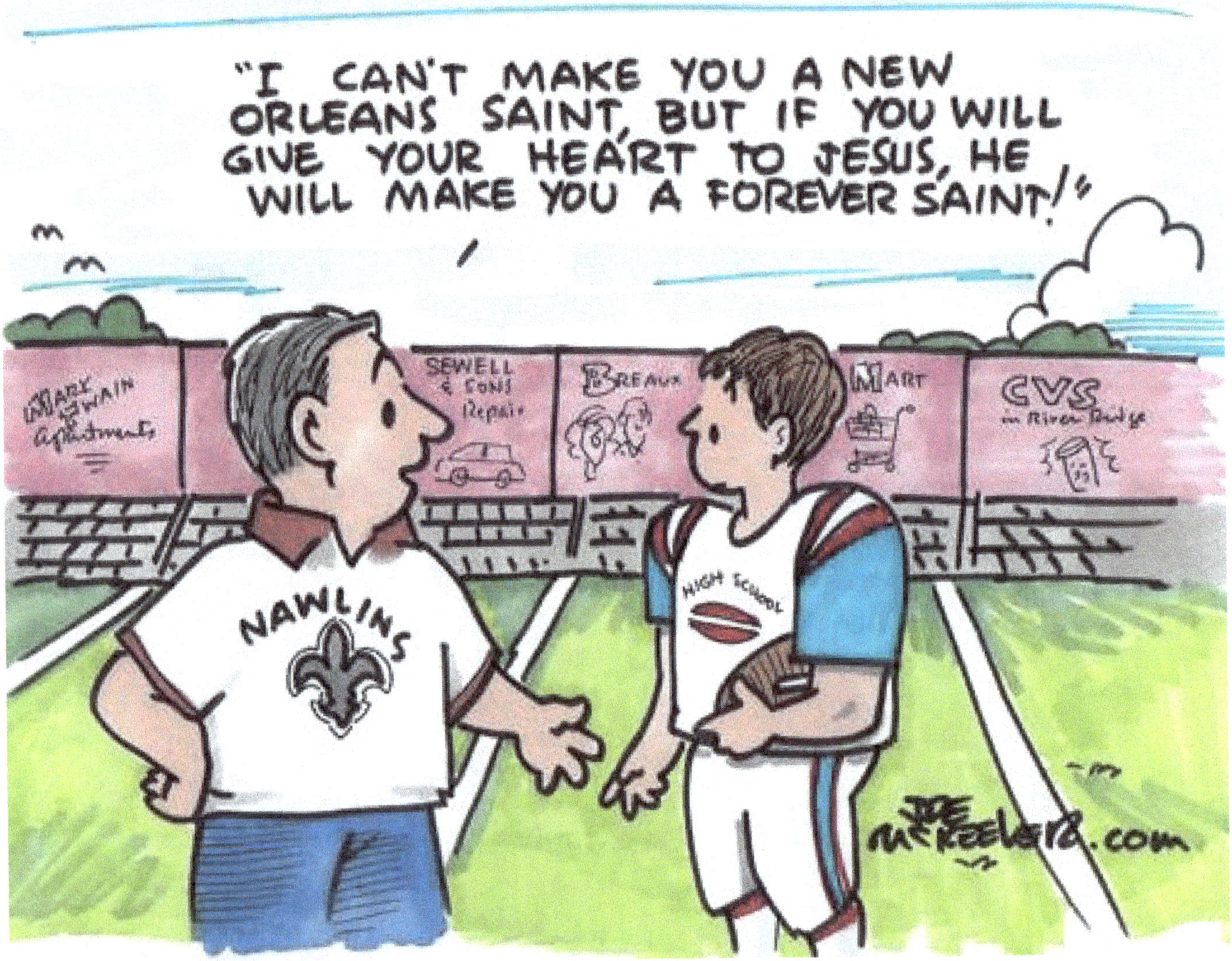
"I CAN'T MAKE YOU A NEW ORLEANS SAINT, BUT IF YOU WILL GIVE YOUR HEART TO JESUS, HE WILL MAKE YOU A FOREVER SAINT!"
SEWELL & SONS Repair
MART
CVS in River Ridge
NAWLINS
HIGH SCHOOL
JOE McKEEVER.com

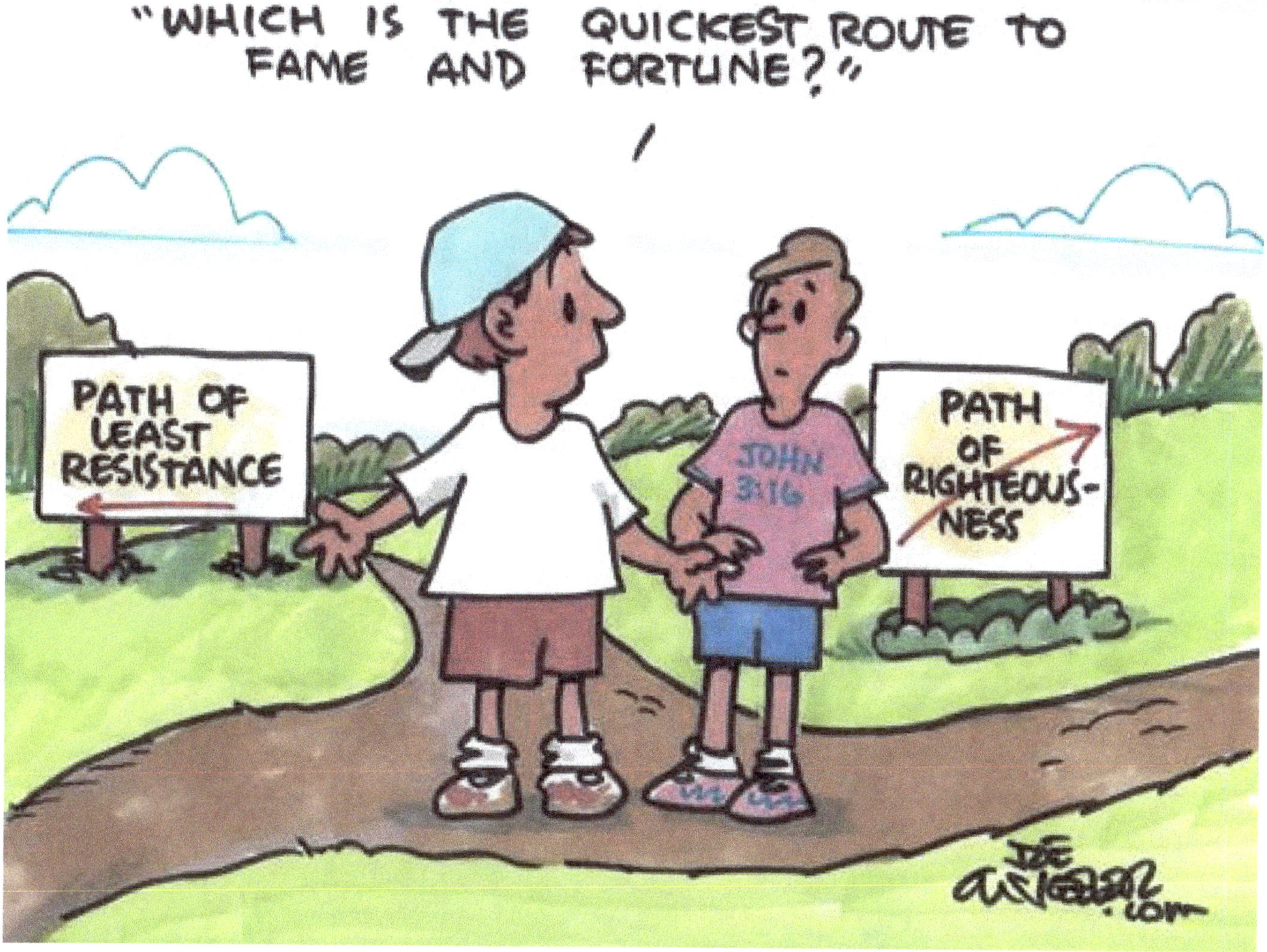
"WHICH IS THE QUICKEST ROUTE TO FAME AND FORTUNE?"
PATH OF LEAST RESISTANCE
JOHN 3:16
PATH OF RIGHTEOUS-NESS

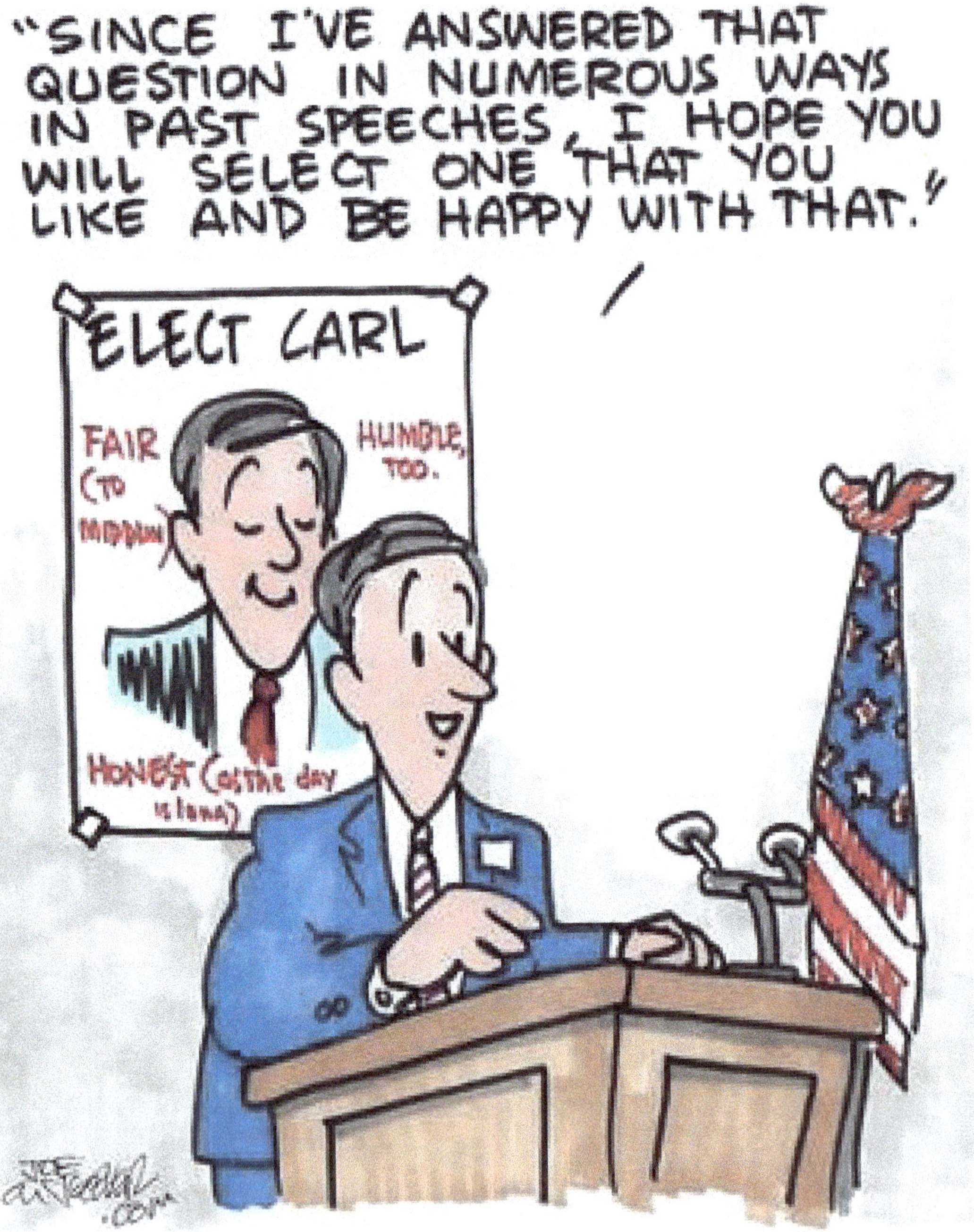
"SINCE I'VE ANSWERED THAT QUESTION IN NUMEROUS WAYS IN PAST SPEECHES, I HOPE YOU WILL SELECT ONE THAT YOU LIKE AND BE HAPPY WITH THAT."
ELECT CARL
FAIR
HUMBLE, TOO.

"MY PASTOR SAYS HE'S RESIGNING TO SPEND MORE TIME WITH THE LORD."

"AND NOW, FOR THE UNDISCIPLINED AND THE INDULGENT IN OUR AUDIENCE, THE FOLLOWING PROGRAM IS RIGHT DOWN YOUR SEWER."

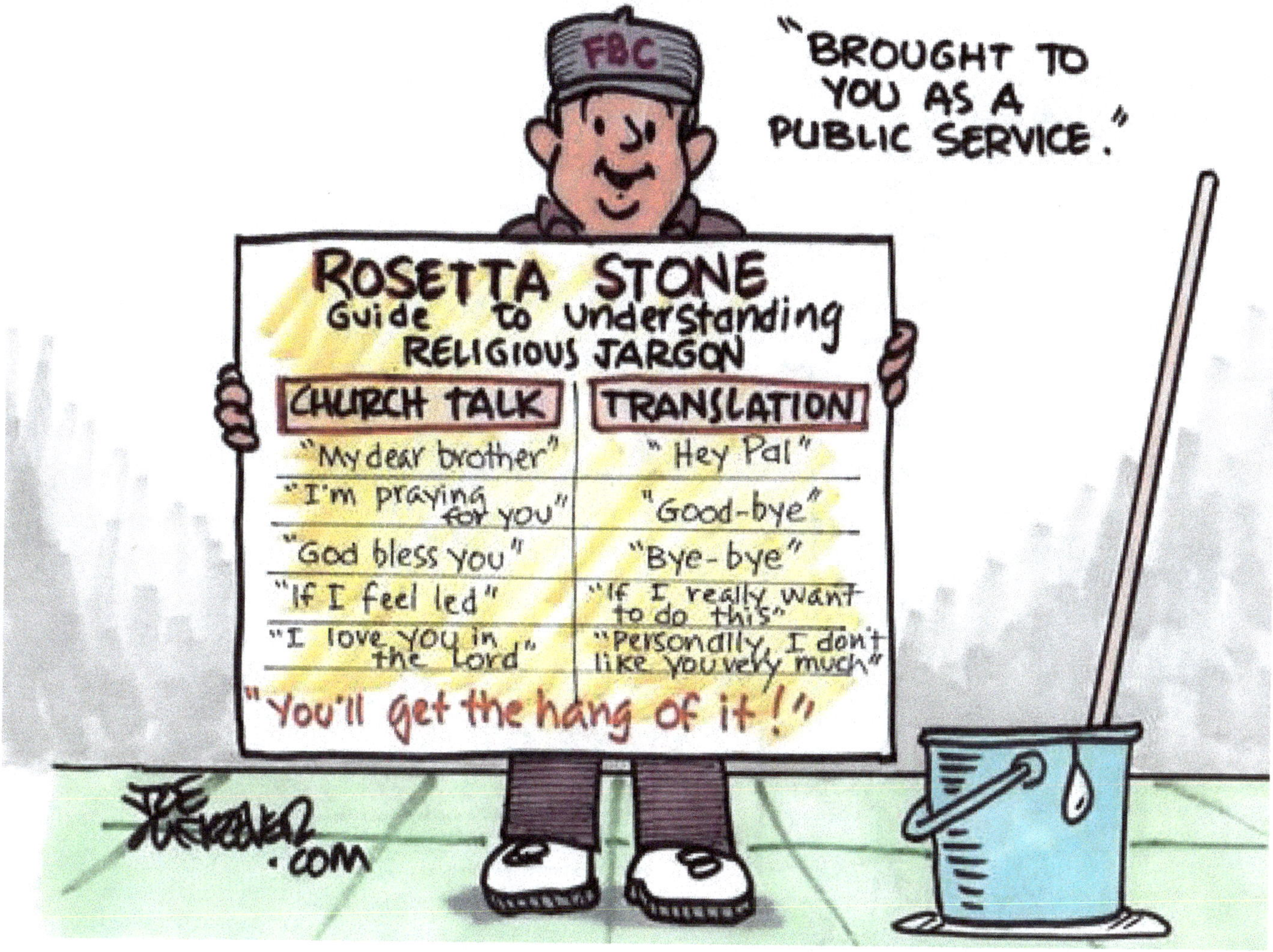
FBC
"BROUGHT TO YOU AS A PUBLIC SERVICE."
ROSETTA STONE
Guide to understanding
RELIGIOUS JARGON
CHURCH TALK
TRANSLATION
"My dear brother"
"Hey Pal"
"I'm praying for you"
"Good-bye"
"God bless you"
"Bye-bye"
"If I feel led"
"If I really want to do this"
"I love you in the Lord"
"Personally, I don't like you very much"
"You'll get the hang of it!"
JOE McKEEVER .com

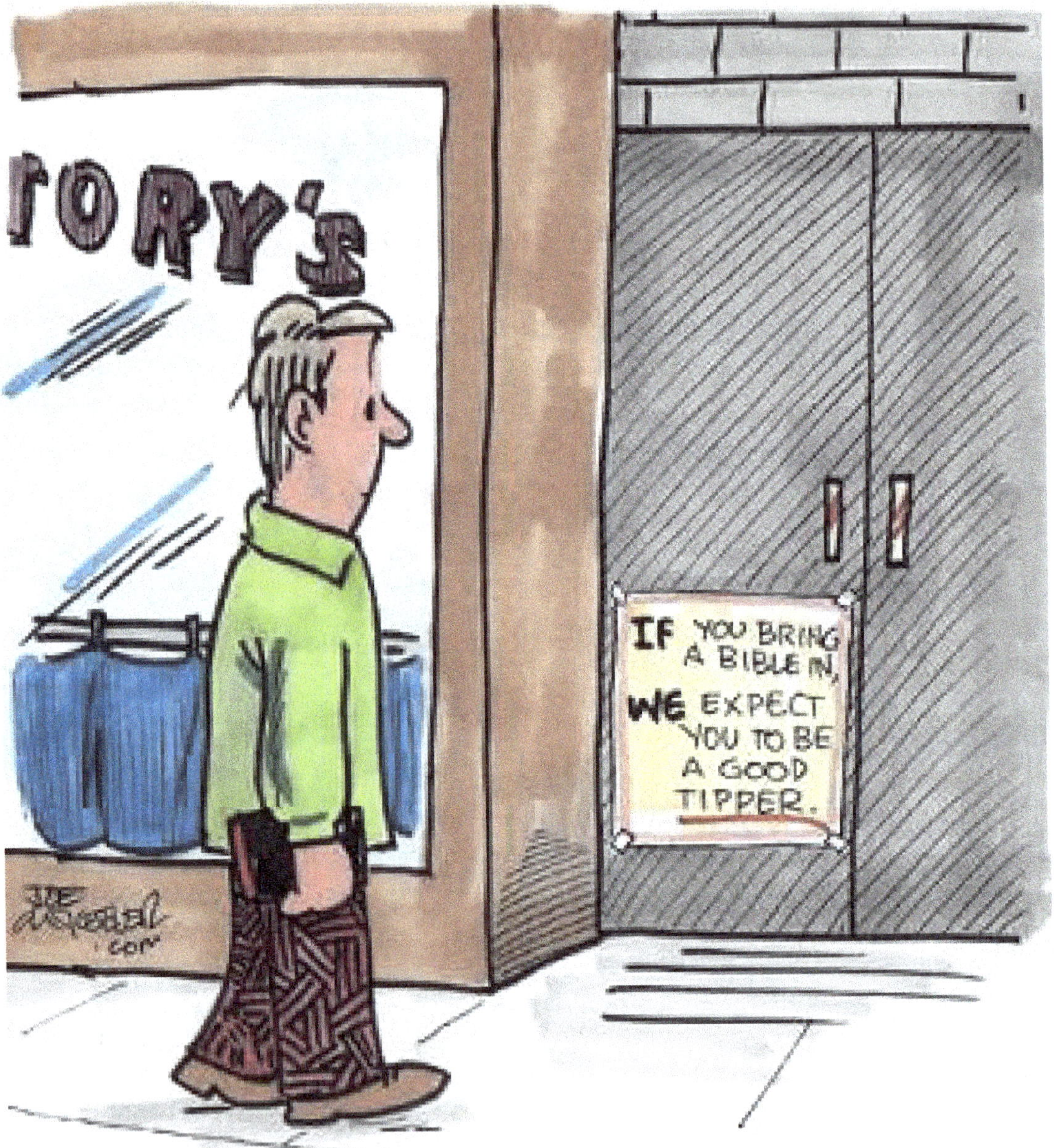
TORY'S
IF YOU BRING A BIBLE IN, WE EXPECT YOU TO BE A GOOD TIPPER.
JOE .com

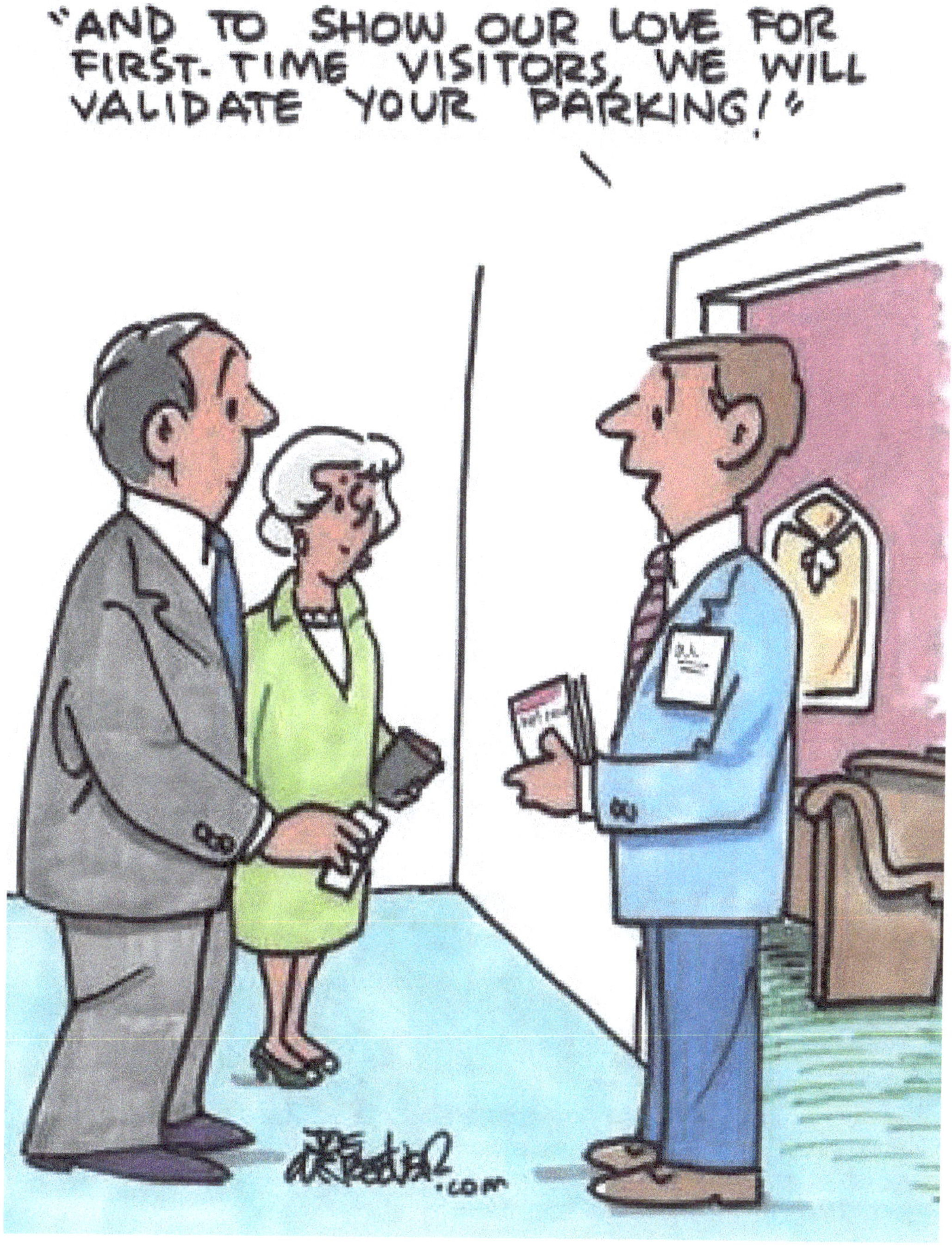
"AND TO SHOW OUR LOVE FOR FIRST-TIME VISITORS, WE WILL VALIDATE YOUR PARKING!"

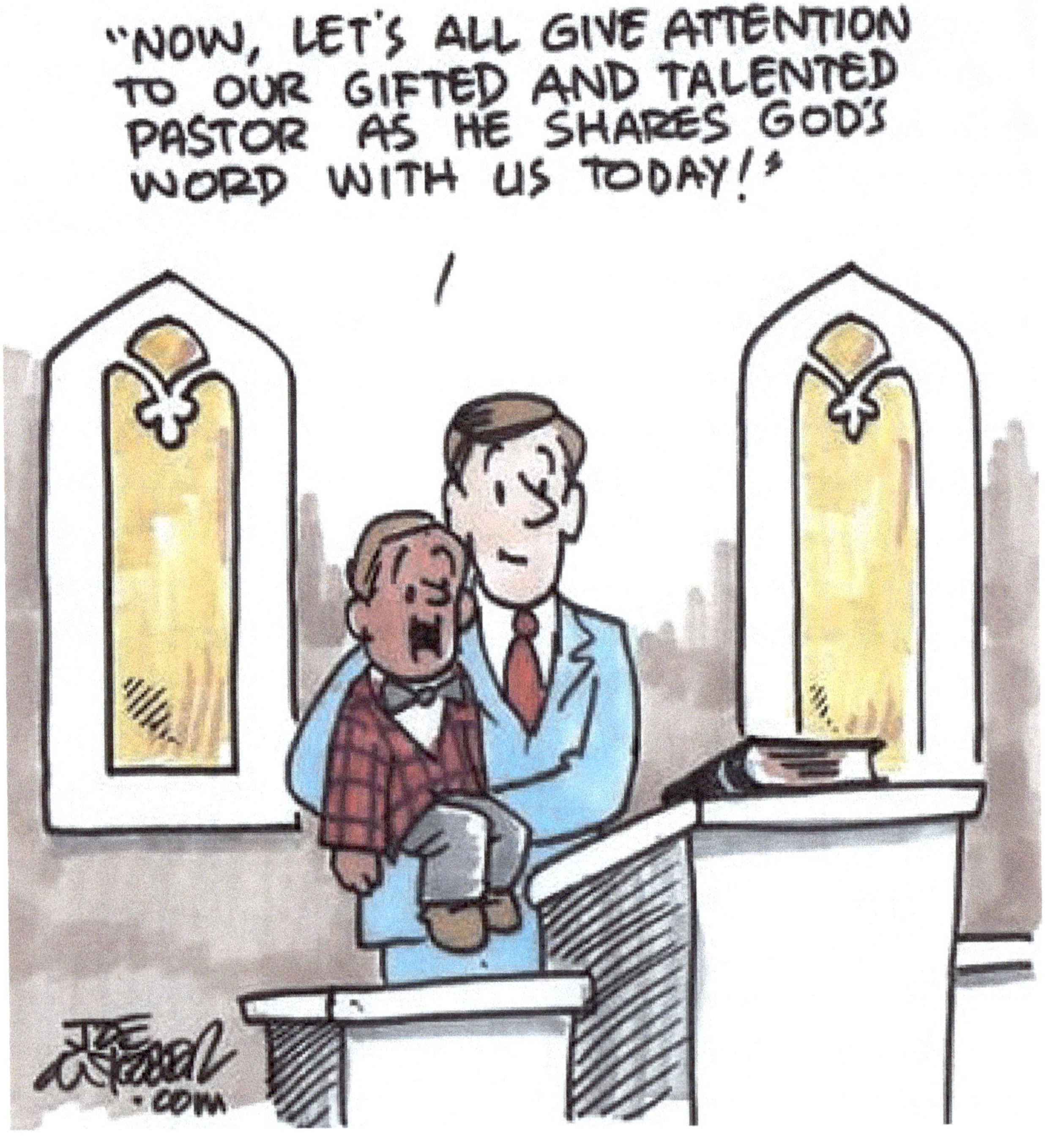
"NOW, LET'S ALL GIVE ATTENTION TO OUR GIFTED AND TALENTED PASTOR AS HE SHARES GOD'S WORD WITH US TODAY!"
JOE MCKEEVER .COM

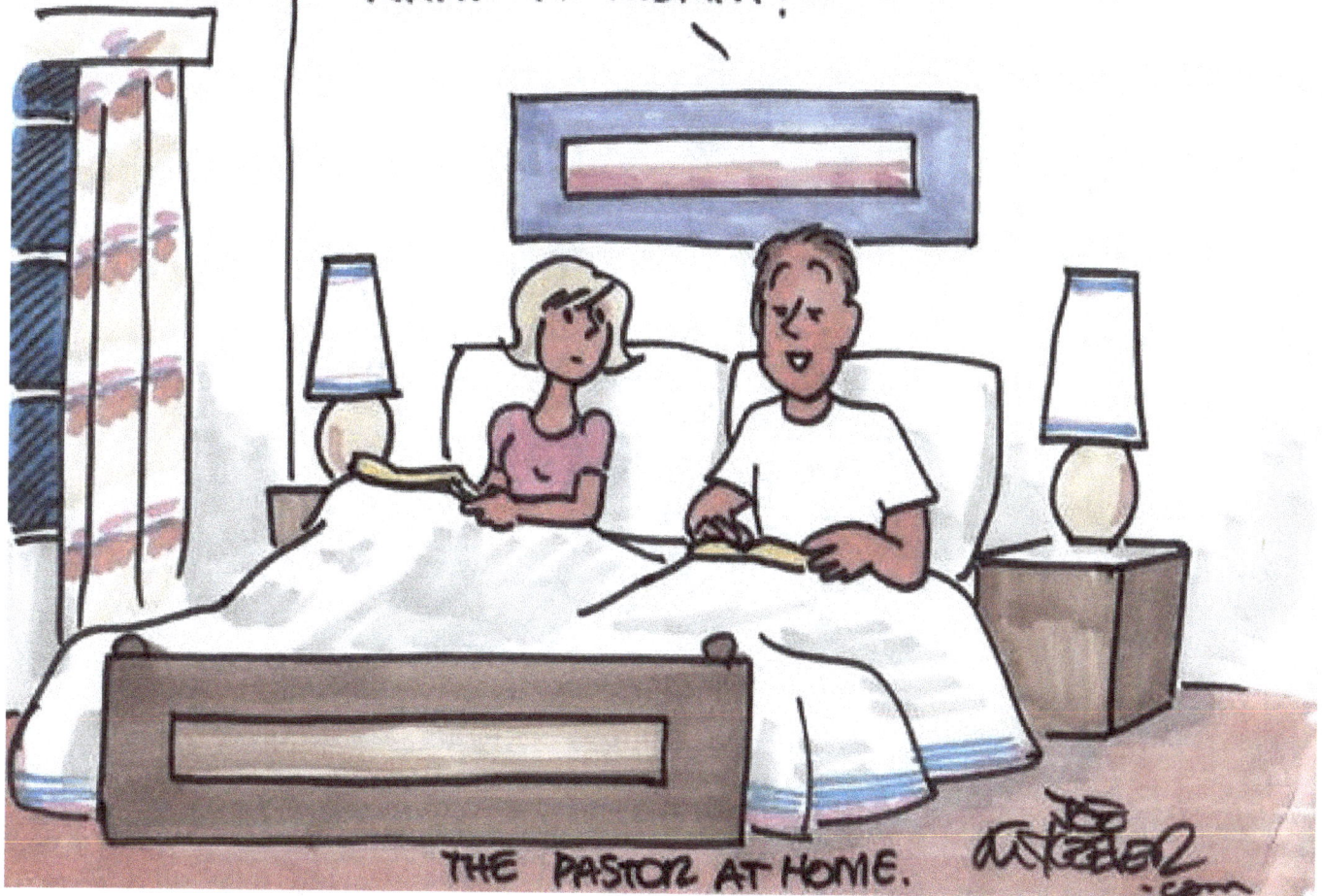

"OH, HERE'S A GOOD TEXT FOR MY SERMON ON CALVINISM. NOW, IF I ONLY KNEW WHAT IT MEANT!"

THE PASTOR AT HOME.

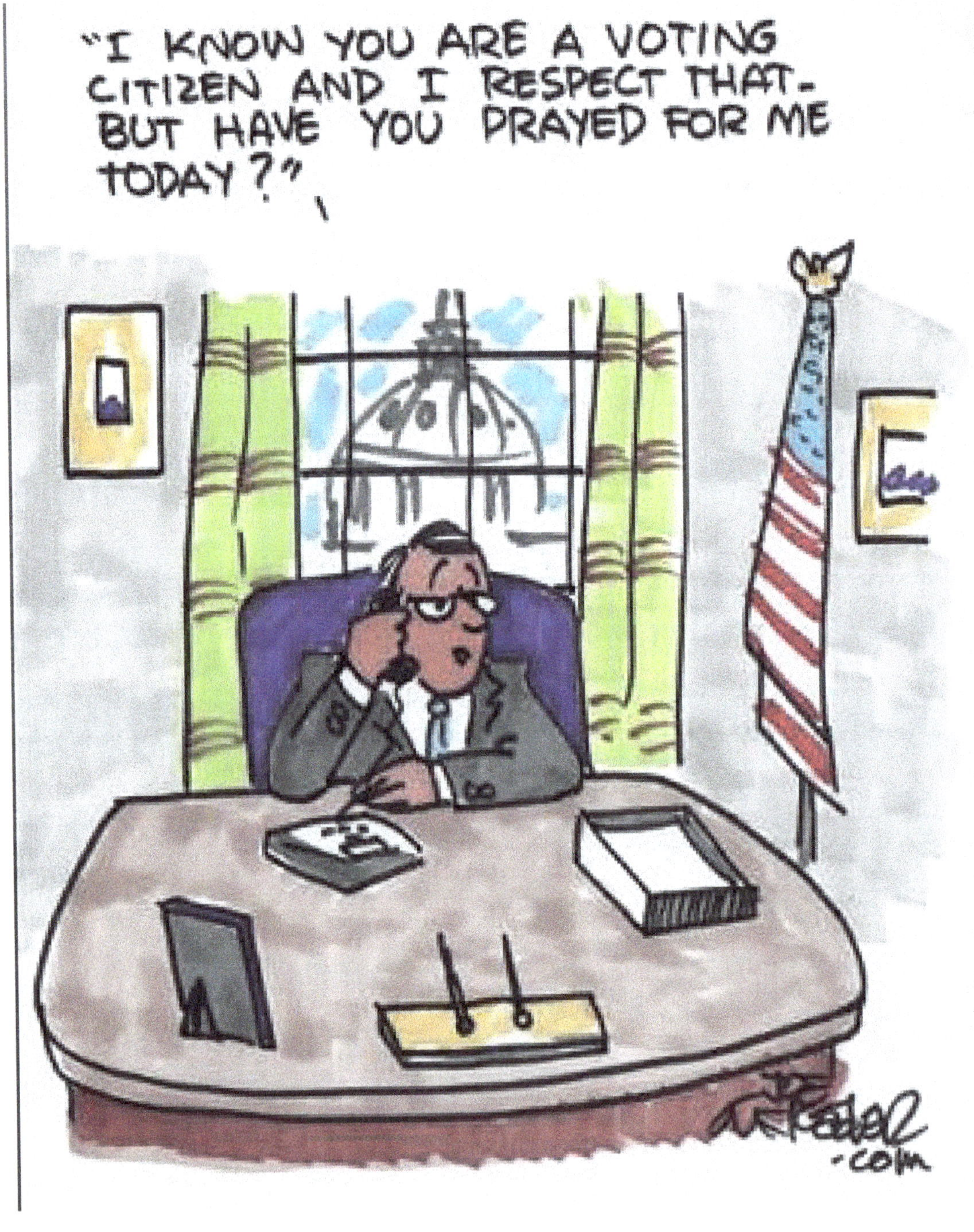
"I KNOW YOU ARE A VOTING CITIZEN AND I RESPECT THAT- BUT HAVE YOU PRAYED FOR ME TODAY?"

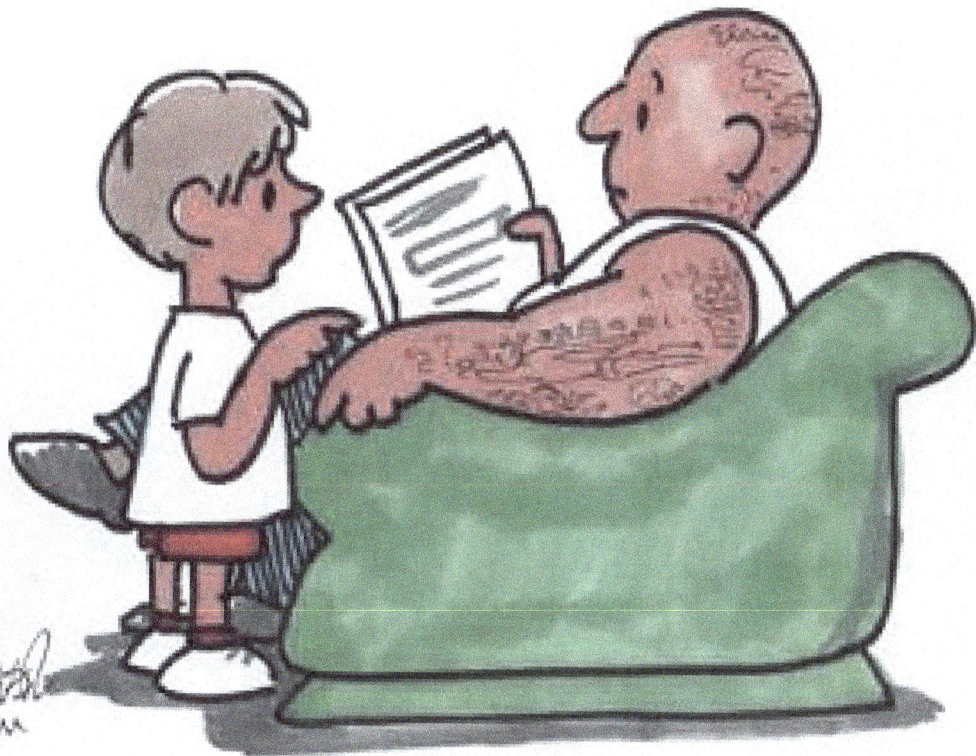
"WHEN CAN I START MY CAREER AS A NEEDLE-POINT SAMPLER LIKE YOU?"

"CALL THE REVEREND. TELL HIM I'M LOSTER THAN I HAVE EVER BEEN IN MY LIFE!"

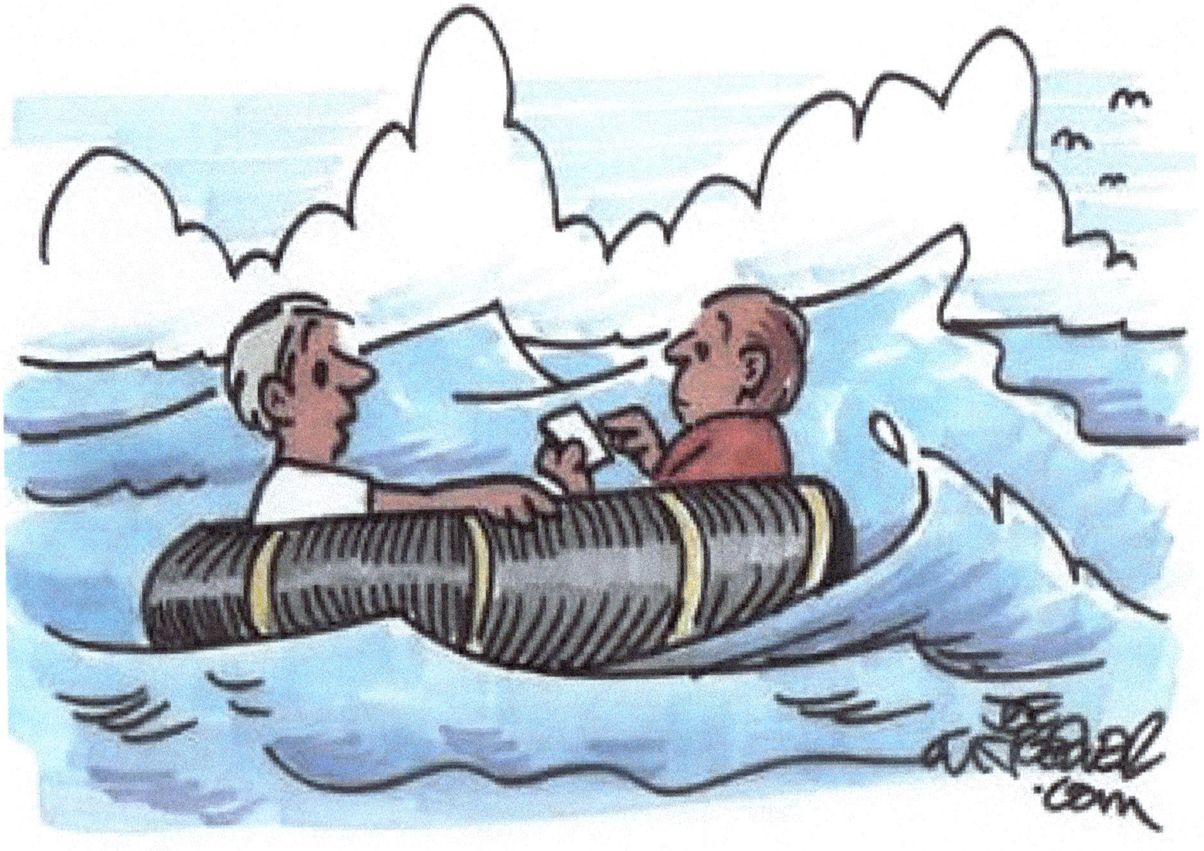

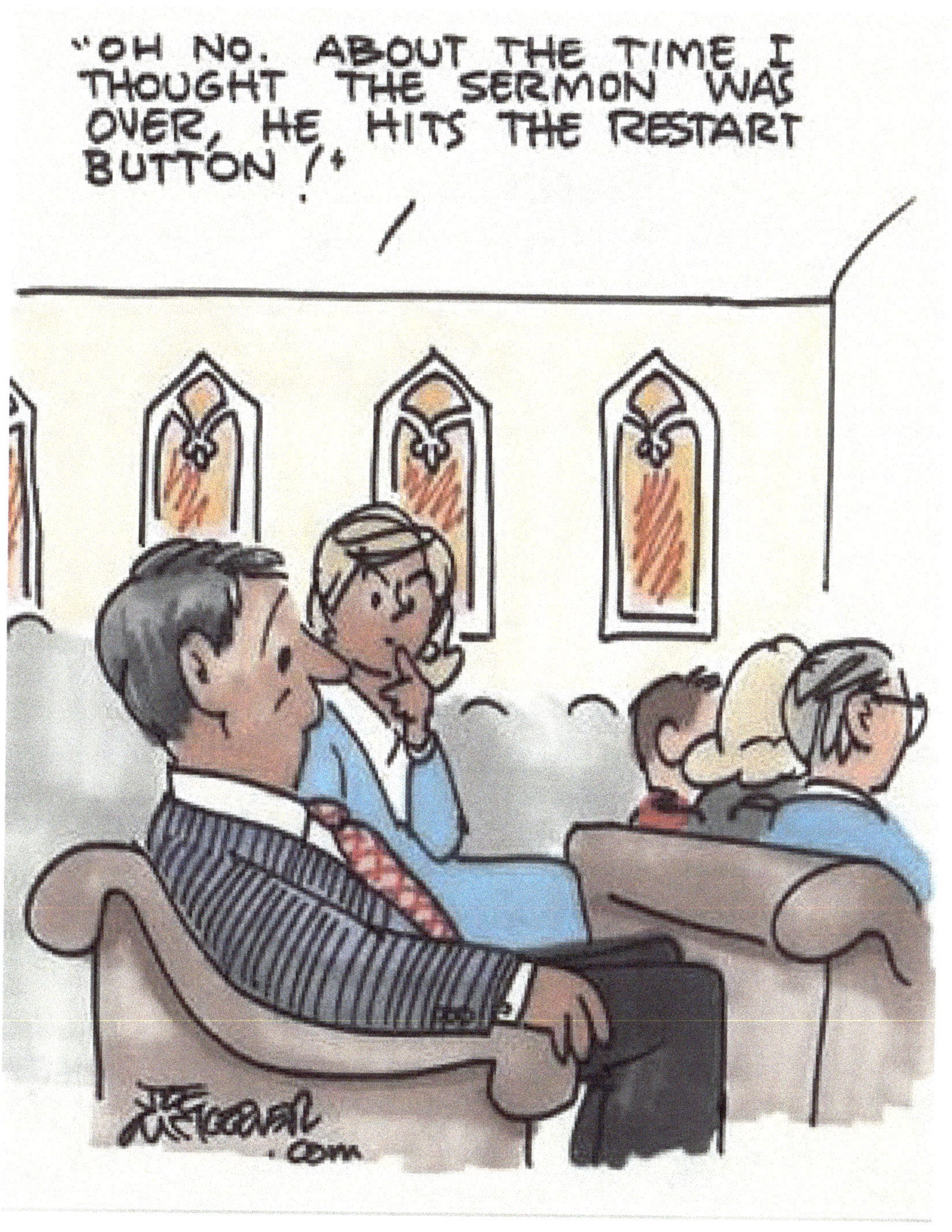
"OH NO. ABOUT THE TIME I THOUGHT THE SERMON WAS OVER, HE HITS THE RESTART BUTTON!"
.com

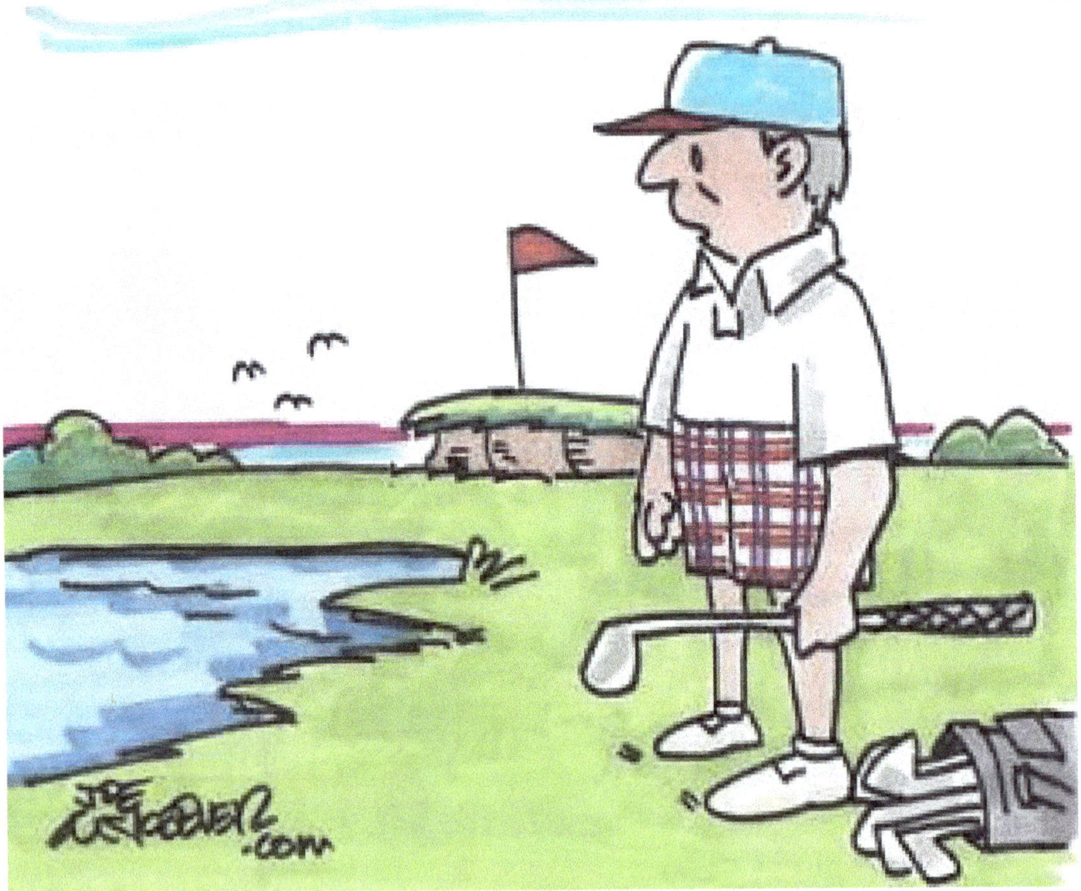

"RIGHT NOW, I COULD USE A GOOD PREACHER, SOMEONE WITH A CALLING TO FIND THE LOST."

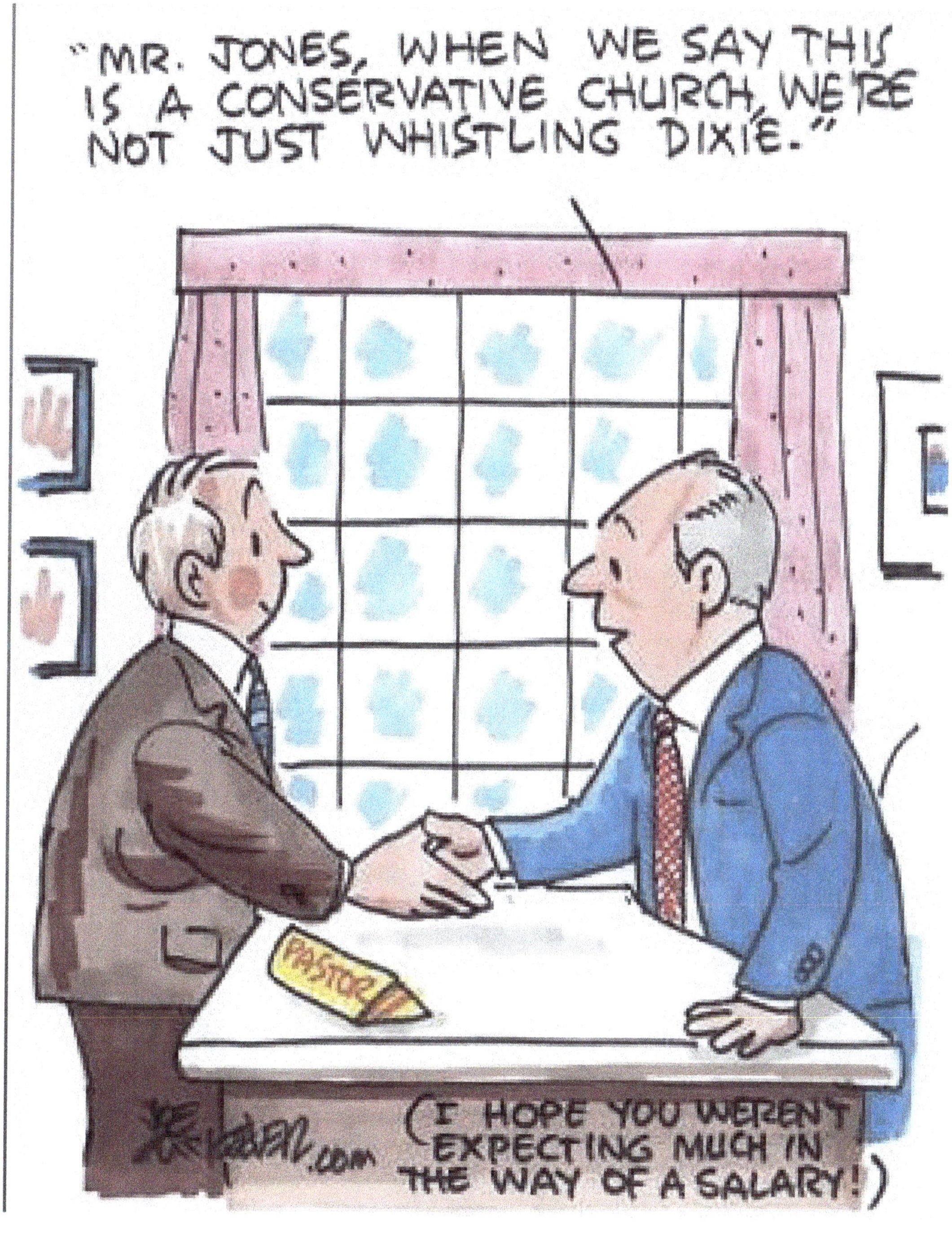
"MR. JONES, WHEN WE SAY THIS IS A CONSERVATIVE CHURCH, WE'RE NOT JUST WHISTLING DIXIE."
PASTOR
(I HOPE YOU WEREN'T EXPECTING MUCH IN THE WAY OF A SALARY!)

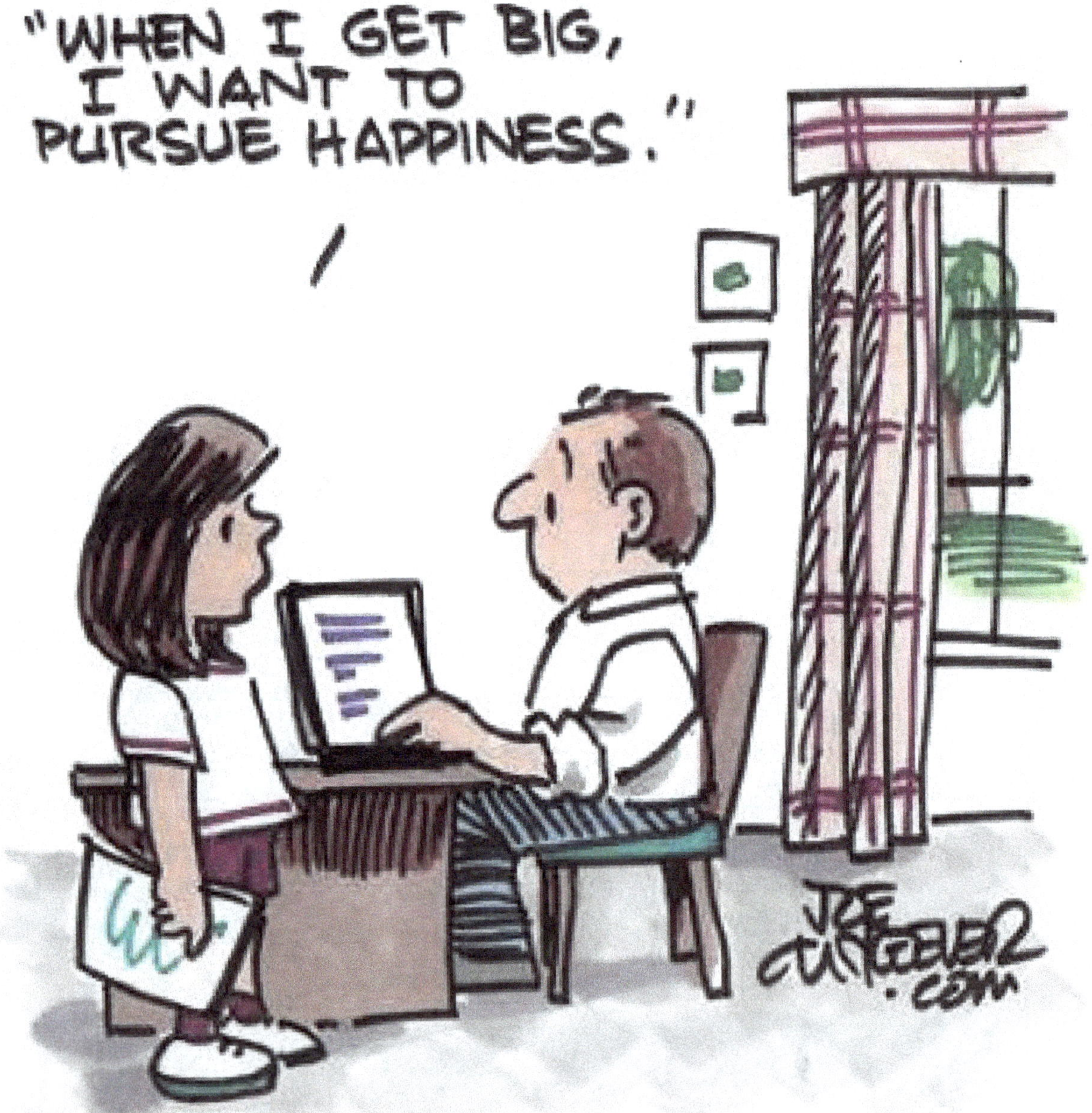
"WHEN I GET BIG, I WANT TO PURSUE HAPPINESS."

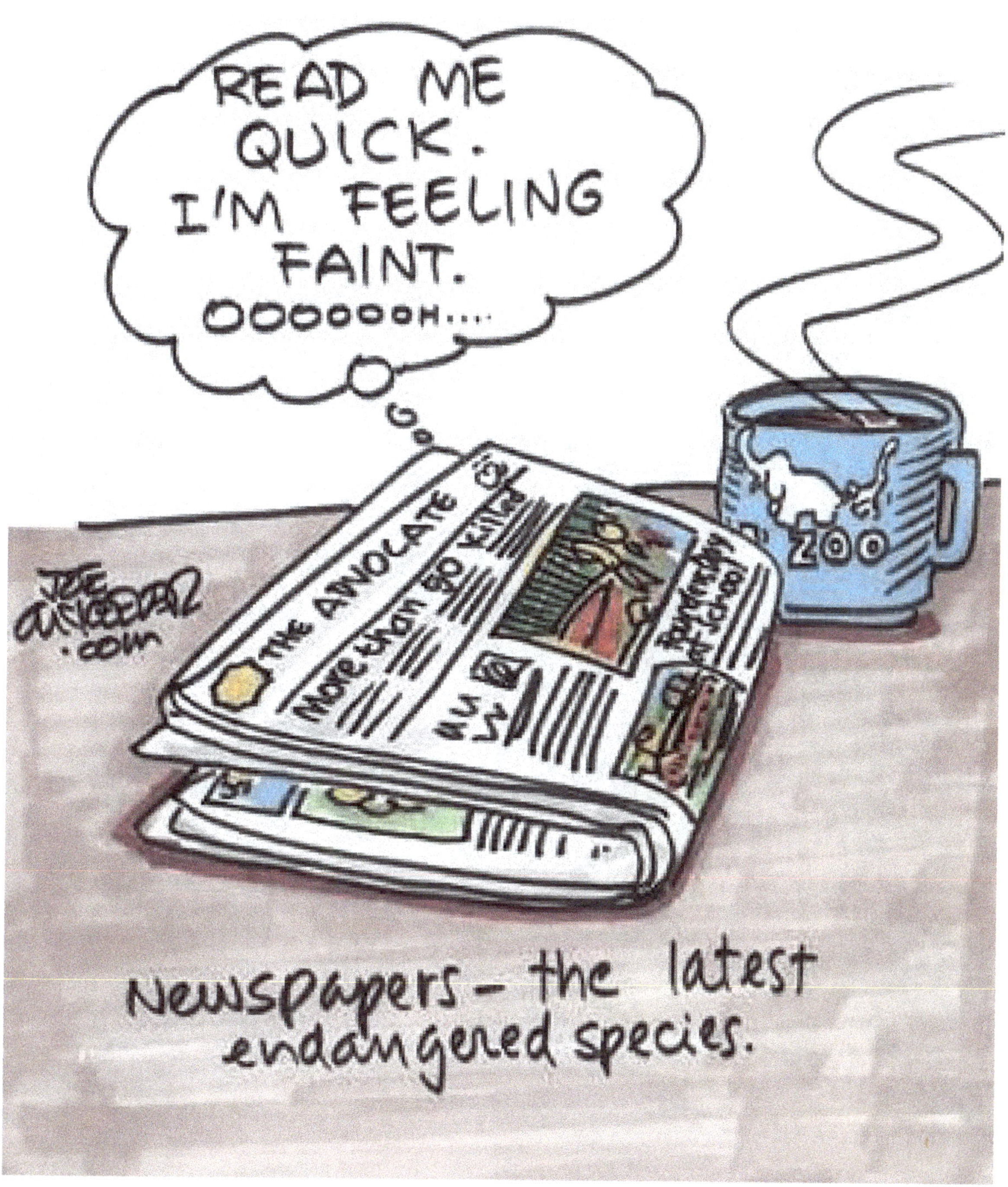
READ ME QUICK. I'M FEELING FAINT. OOOOOOOH....
THE ADVOCATE
ZOO
Newspapers - the latest endangered species.

"LORD, YOU STILL AWAKE? I NEED TO TALK TO SOMEBODY AND YOU'RE THE ONLY ONE WHO ISN'T ASLEEP."

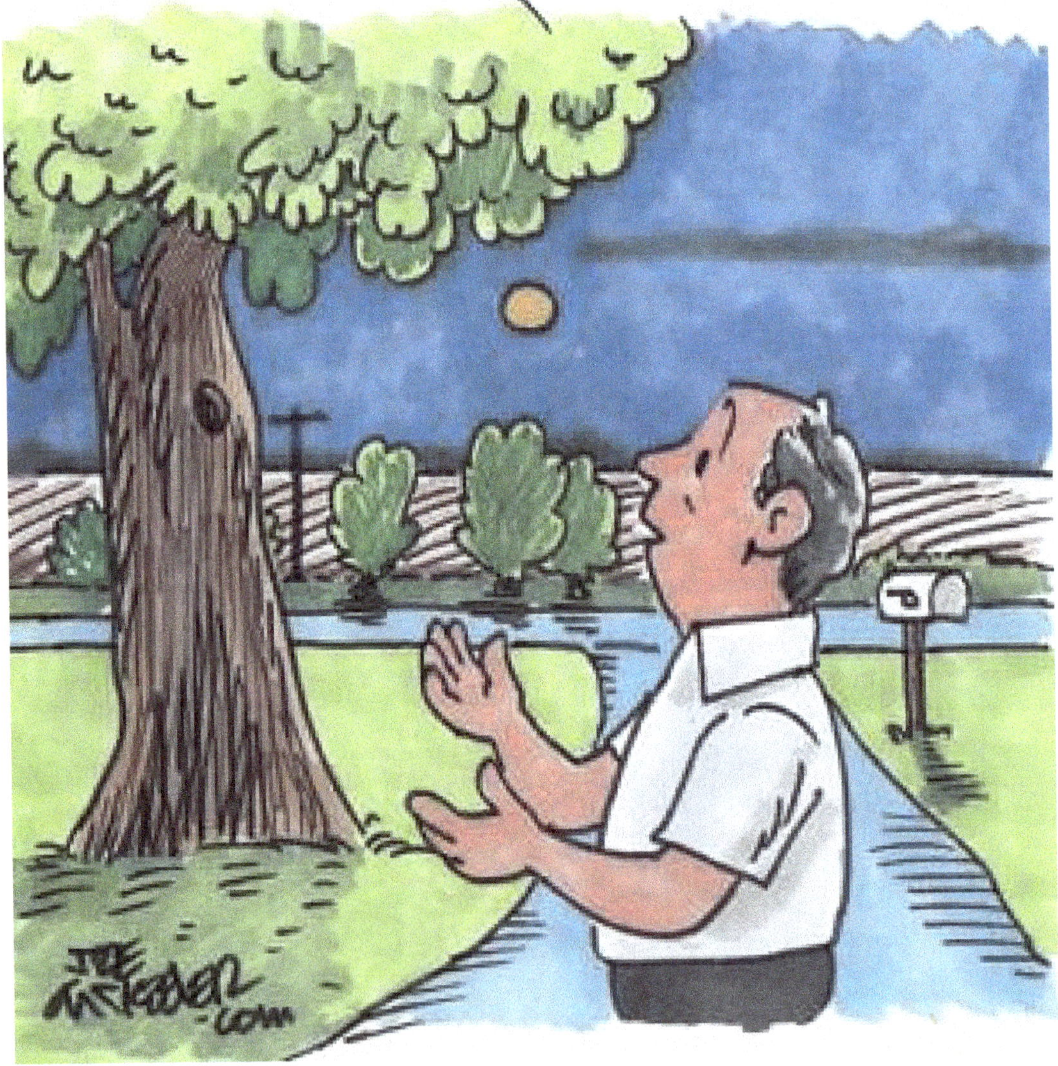

"SORRY TO GET YOU OUT TONIGHT, CHIEF— BUT MY LITTLE CHURCH IS IN NEED OF SOME TITHERS AND YOU ARE KNOWN FOR FINDING YOUR MAN!"

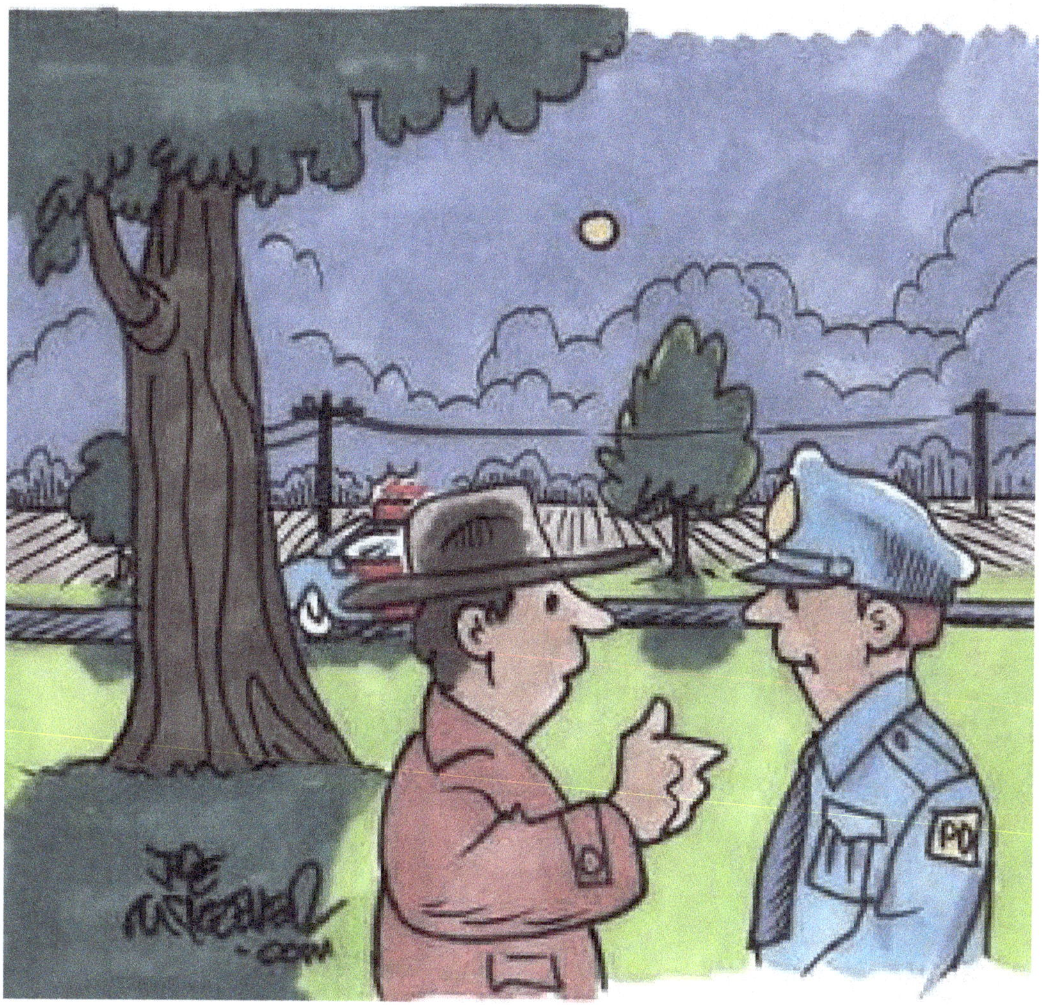
PD

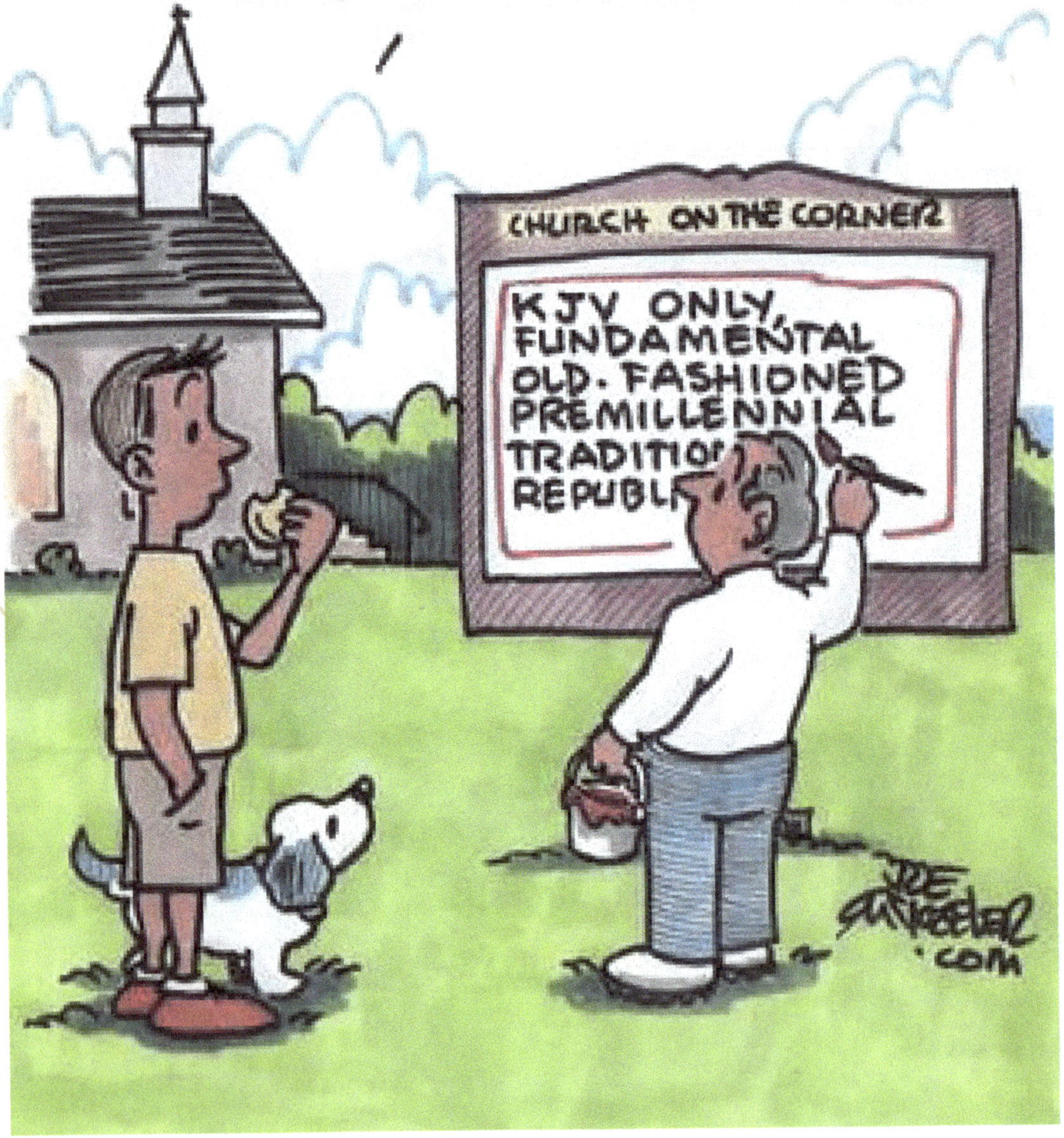
CHURCH ON THE CORNER
KJV ONLY,
FUNDAMENTAL
OLD-FASHIONED
PREMILLENNIAL
TRADITION
REPUBL

"I'LL BET IF YOU TRIED, YOU COULD THINK OF MORE WAYS TO EXCLUDE PEOPLE."

"YOUR SERMON ON THE END OF THE WORLD WOULD BE HELPED BY SOME LIGHT-HEARTED STORIES AND A JOKE OR TWO."

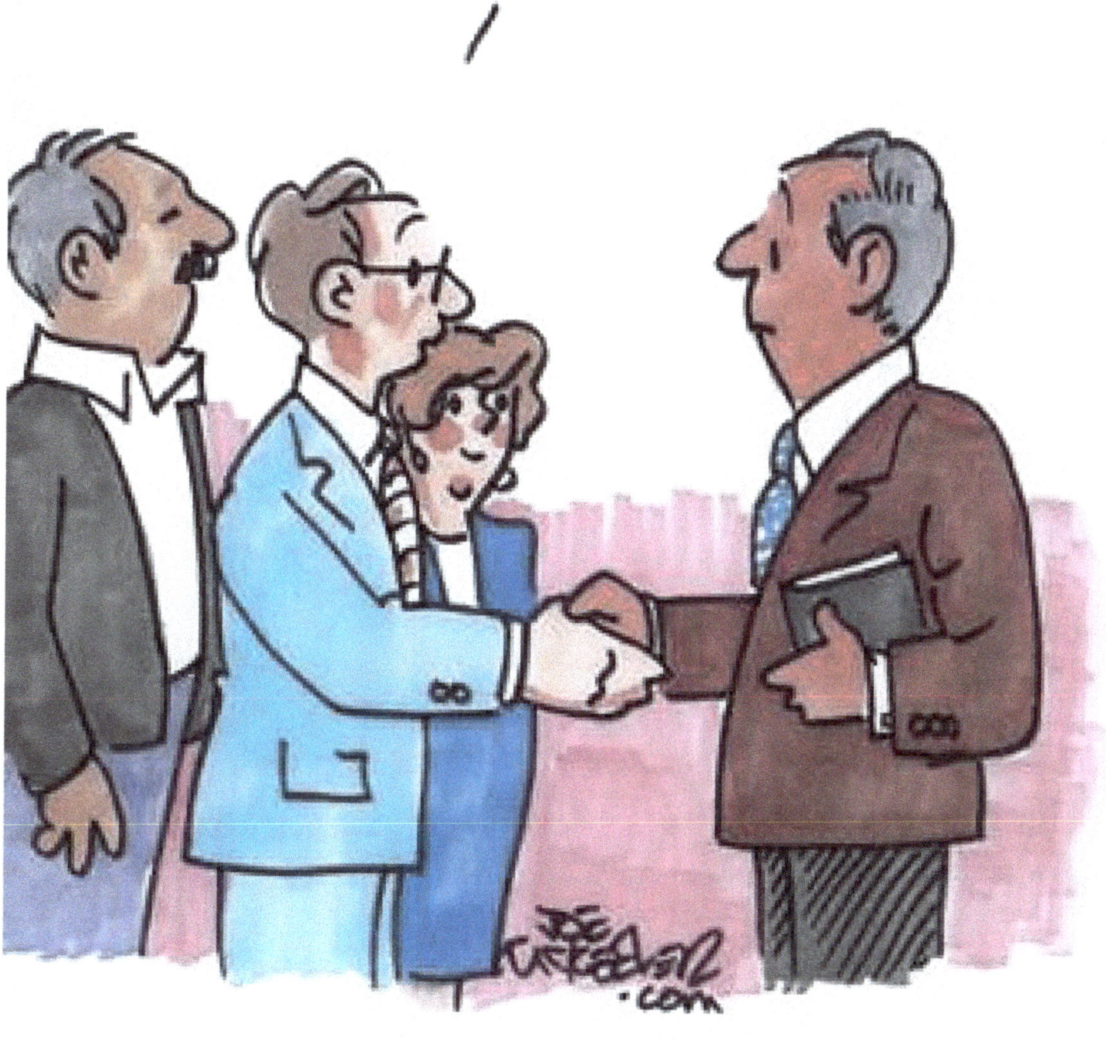

www.ingramcontent.com/pod-product-compliance
Lightning Source LLC
Chambersburg PA
CBHW081543040426

42448CB00015B/3203